SELECTED POEMS OF
ROBERT BROWNING

ROBERT BROWNING IN 1858
From the painting by M. Gordigiani

SELECTED POEMS OF
ROBERT BROWNING

Edited with an Introduction
and Notes
by

JAMES REEVES

HEINEMANN

LONDON

Heinemann Educational Books Ltd
LONDON MELBOURNE TORONTO
SINGAPORE CAPE TOWN
AUCKLAND IBADAN
HONG KONG

ROBERT BROWNING 1812–1889

FIRST PUBLISHED 1955
REPRINTED 1959, 1961, 1962, 1964

Published by
Heinemann Educational Books Ltd
15–16 Queen Street, Mayfair, London, W.1
Printed in Great Britain by Morrison & Gibb Ltd
London and Edinburgh

CONTENTS

Introduction

ROBERT BROWNING
(1812–1889)

I

THE POSITION OF BROWNING TO-DAY

On the last day of 1889 Robert Browning was buried in Poets'
Corner in Westminster Abbey. The position thus accorded him
by public opinion has since then been very strenuously chal-
lenged. Elderly people whose minds were formed during the
period of Browning's highest reputation are loud in his defence
against a younger generation, now middle-aged, who have
allowed their idol's name to fall into disrepute. They are exultant
at signs of a Browning revival. A still younger generation is
puzzled to know what to make of the voluminous and scarcely
accessible master who has been variously compared with
Chaucer, whom they admire, and dismissed as a bore, philistine,
optimist, and even something of a humbug.

It is largely for the generation of the puzzled that the present
selection has been made. Anyone anxious to discover Browning
has the formidable task of finding out where to begin amidst
the fifteen hundred closely printed columns of the collected
poems. A reader of poetry brought up on, say, Donne, Marvell,
Blake, Keats, and Hopkins—who are known and admired
principally for short poems of incomparable beauty and, in the
main compressed, almost gnomic, utterance—may be wearied
by Browning's apparently inexhaustible *longueurs*, his narrative
garrulity, his prolix prosiness. They may have read Oscar
Wilde's remark, 'Meredith is a prose Browning, and so is
Browning. He used poetry as a medium for writing in prose.'[1]

[1] *Intentions* ('The Critic as Artist').

They may object to being button-holed by a familiar old gentle-man with a long tongue but, alas! no glittering eye, and forced to listen to two or three thousand lines of doubtful medieval history. They do not perhaps find the usual anthology pieces quite convincing evidence of the greatness ascribed to Browning. Yet they have a strong feeling that, somewhere amidst the medieval bric-à-brac, the prosiness, the grotesque rhymes, the flat blank verse, the frequent exhortations towards an ill-defined upward-striving, a poet lies hidden. A writer of this younger generation concludes an interesting article on Browning with the opinion that he was 'a genuine but not a great poet'.[1] I hope that the genuine poet may be found in the present selection.

The question of Browning's 'greatness' must be left aside: our notions of what constitutes this elusive quality are under-going continual change. I doubt whether he can be called 'great' for our time, in the sense in which Donne and Blake are great. It would be difficult to name a single poem of Browning's which would at present find general acceptance as revealing unmistakably the accent of greatness. What might be more acceptable, perhaps, is the idea of Browning as a *major* poet, in a sense in which neither Donne nor Blake is major. Browning was much more a man of his age; his failings as poet may partly be traced to the non-poetic, even anti-poetic, nature of that age. The nineteenth century was materialistic in so far as its imaginative needs were answered, not by poetry, but by the novel, which in those days meant, among other things, an accumulation of material detail. In trying to come to terms with the imaginative demands of his age, Browning made poetry approach more nearly to the novel than anyone else since Chaucer. There is that force at least in the comparison. But the genuine poet was almost irretrievably submerged in the novelist; there is at least that much force in Wilde's epigram. The Victorians were prepared to read poetry—new poetry, that

---

[1] *Essays in Criticism*, Vol. III., No. 2, April 1953. 'Robert Browning—a Potential Revolutionary', by J. A. Boulton.

is—on their own terms: they accepted Tennyson, on condition that his outlook could be squared with middle-class morality; they accepted Browning, when he was over fifty and had left all dangerously anti-social ideas behind, or at any rate could be trusted to conceal them under the now proverbial cloak of his 'obscurity'.

Browning is a major poet in the sense that he is still, and may always be, disputable. His poems will, for many years to come, find new explorers, and they will make fresh discoveries in the immense hinterland of the poems and dramas which others have found unreadable. He is a major poet in the sense that, even where he will not be explored, he cannot be ignored. It is impossible to sum up his achievement in a neat phrase.

Provided we can read long poems at all, we can often find Browning readable, even when we are not sure what we are reading him for. We know we do not read his long poems for the sort of poetic experience we get from Donne or Blake; yet we feel that the most admired poets in our time are not necessarily the sole inheritors of poetic greatness. We may only be reading Browning 'for the story' or for the revelation of a 'character'. We know that we have sometimes read Chaucer, and perhaps even Shakespeare, for the same things. In any case, it is Browning's story, told in his way, that we enjoy; and it would certainly not be the same story told in any other way. If we read the comparatively short poems of Donne, or Marvell, or Hardy, for the poetic 'moment', we may, while admitting that there are few, if any, such moments in Browning, nevertheless be prepared to enlarge our conception of poetry to include some at least of Browning's characteristic qualities.

These qualities are fully illustrated in the pages which follow. An editor may perhaps be forgiven, in the case of Browning, for making something of a 'personal' selection, since it can, in any case, be only an introduction. Once it is known that he has embarked on the editing of a Browning selection, all his friends and acquaintances express the hope that he will include this or that from among their own favourites. He soon finds that if he acceded in every case, his selection would get out of hand. Critics have proclaimed as Browning's 'masterpiece' more than one poem which does not seem to me even worthy of inclusion. Every reader of Browning, it seems, makes his personal selection, and depends very little on the judgment of others. This is evidence, not only of Browning's fascination, but also that no selection could possibly claim to be authoritative. I have naturally included as much of what seems to me the best of Browning as could be got into the available space. If I have inevitably omitted the favourite poem of scores of Browning's admirers, it has been with the sincere intention of making an acceptable selection for readers anxious to discover the genuine poet, not the young revolutionary, the metaphysician, the psychologist, or the apostle of progress.

II

EARLY LIFE AND POEMS

Robert Browning was born in May 1812 at Camberwell, on the outskirts of London. His father, the son of a West Indian slave-owner, forbidden the life of an artist, which he desired, had become a clerk in the Bank of England. He was a delightful man and, in reaction against the tyranny of his own father, an indulgent parent. He was unambitious, disliked his work, and lived for his artistic and intellectual interests. He was a fluent and talented versifier. His wife, of mixed German and Scottish parentage, was devout and neurotic. In religion the Brownings were Congregationalist. Besides their son Robert, they had one daughter, Sarianna; she never married, but kept house for her father after her mother's death; then, after her father's death, she lived with her brother Robert, by this time a widower. The formative influences in Robert's childhood were his father's books, of which there were thousands, and his emotional dependence on his mother. He attended a local school, and left at fourteen. After that, his education was almost entirely informal. He had no addiction to regular learning, but preferred to browse among the curiosities of the library at home. He conceived a taste for keeping strange pets, which persisted all his life. Among the animals he encouraged were toads, spiders, lizards, a bat, an owl and two geese. He found time to make a reasonably close acquaintance with the classics, and even attended some lectures on Greek at London University, until he found the discomforts of lodgings too great after the comforts of home.

He lived with his parents until his marriage at the age of thirty-four. His attachment to home was centred on his relations with his mother, from whom he derived a nervous irritability which lasted well into manhood. When she was unwell, his own health suffered correspondingly.

Of Browning's early life Osbert Burdett wrote: 'None of his energies was wasted in rebellion, and the life of Browning is a valuable example of a man of genius allowed to unfold without external interference.'[1] But an absence of external conflict is often offset by inner divisions, and his latest biographer[2] finds evidence of a spiritual and emotional crisis in adolescence which profoundly affected his subsequent development. At the age of fourteen Browning discovered Shelley. The impact was not unlike what would have been felt by a boy in similar circumstances who discovered D. H. Lawrence in 1930. Regarded by respectable middle-class nonconformist circles as an atheist, blasphemer and social outcast, Shelley appealed instantly to this intelligent, restless boy as a champion of liberty and a leader of revolt against convention and oppression. Byron had been his first love in poetry, and it is no doubt the influence of Byron's comic style which gave to his later idiom its peculiar colloquial flavour. It was Shelley's style, however, which Browning

---

[1] Osbert Burdett, *The Brownings* (Constable), 1928.
[2] Betty Miller, *Robert Browning: a Portrait* (Murray), 1952.

imitated in his earliest surviving work. It was the example of Shelley which fired him to dedicate his life to poetry, in the hope of making some striking contribution to the progress of intellectual freedom and the perfection of man.

But this new passion brought him into sharp conflict with his mother, whose sternly orthodox religious notions made her regard Shelley's ideas with horror. Emotionally, it seems, Browning capitulated to his mother; his love of Shelley, though not disavowed in any dramatic way, was driven underground. In any case, if he was to devote himself to poetry, he had to live at home; his father gave in to his unwillingness to try for a post in the Bank of England, and encouraged his literary ambition, maintaining him until his marriage and paying for the publication of his poems. Browning never had to work for money. His home life was singularly harmonious and uneventful; such an atmosphere, if we are to judge from our knowledge of the lives of other poets, is not necessarily the best for the unfolding of genius, which may find its sharpest incentive in conflict and rebellion. Outward harmony and goodwill may have the effect of making a sensitive child secretive; certainly Browning associated a feeling of guilt with his continuing reverence for Shelley, whose inspiration he came to feel he had in some way betrayed. This is the theme of the first poem he published. *Pauline* appeared when he was not quite twenty-one. It is a long tribute to Shelley, in Shelleyan style, and a confession of his own unworthiness.[1] All his earlier juvenilia were destroyed, and he tried later to suppress the remaining copies of *Pauline*, which he was accustomed to dismiss as a mere literary curiosity.

This poem, although a failure, aroused the interest of a few critics of discernment. J. S. Mill wrote with distaste of the poet's 'intense and morbid self-consciousness'. It is, indeed, a

---

[1] This poem, though of remarkable biographical interest and considerable promise, is quite uncharacteristic of the mature Browning. It is too long to be included in full, but two significant passages, both about Shelley, are given as an appendix (p. 129).

highly subjective poem—'a fragment of a confession', as its sub-title runs. Stung by the effect of his own self-exposure, Browning came to regard introspective writing as unmanly. His next poem, *Paracelsus* (1835), has for its real theme his ambition as a poet, but its meaning was so disguised as to baffle the critics; and it is clear that the 'morbid' subjectivity of *Pauline*, had, in two years, shocked him into the self-concealment which became habitual. Of this more will be said later. The fact to be grasped for the understanding of Browning's growth as a poet is that the realisation of what Shelley stood for involved him in evasion and secrecy. Shelley stood for the individual, for the supremacy of personal volition, for intellectual freedom and the necessity of following the poet's vision, wherever it might lead. In Shelley's case it had led to an early death; in Browning's case it seemed to be leading to failure as a poet and to rebellion against a society to which, as it was represented by the home at Camberwell, he felt himself emotionally and temperamentally attached by unbreakable bonds. It is interesting to recall, briefly, his subsequent relations with his original source of inspiration: when he was forty he attempted, in a preface to some spurious letters of Shelley, to vindicate him as an essentially religious being, one who would have become Christian if he had lived, but in old age he repudiated him completely, refusing in 1886 the presidency of the Shelley society on the ground that he could not approve of Shelley's moral character.

In 1840 Browning published *Sordello*, which caused critics unprecedented bewilderment, and has always been proverbial for extreme obscurity.[1] It is, like the two previous poems, concerned with the problem of the artist's relation to society. The actual subject is deliberately remote from contemporary life, and historically vague. Browning has always been charged

---

[1] Mrs. Carlyle, for example, found the poem interesting, but wished to know whether Sordello was a man, or a city, or a book. Tennyson said that the first line ('Who will, may hear Sordello's story told') and the last line ('Who would, has heard Sordello's story told') were the only two lines in the poem which he understood, and they were lies.

with obscurity, but his obscurity is really evasiveness. His logical meaning can usually be disentangled with a little patience, but its poetic significance—the question of what the poet is 'getting at'—is often not so easily determined.

During the years of his early manhood Browning had, as we have seen, been able to live a life devoted to poetry and free from material cares. He began to be known in literary and artistic circles as a writer of promise. He was handsome, and something of a dandy. Anxious for a wider popularity than his poems were earning him, he made the acquaintance of the celebrated actor Macready, for whom, in 1837, he composed a tragedy in blank verse on the subject of Strafford. It was a failure, yet Browning continued, for a good many years, to be attracted to the theatre. The weakness of all his plays is that he could not portray character in action. This is the essence of the drama, and without it no play can have the wide popular appeal that success in the theatre requires.

In 1838 he made his first journey across Europe to Venice, where he conceived that love of Italy which played so important a part in his later life. In 1841 he published *Pippa Passes* as No. I of a series of pamphlets entitled *Bells and Pomegranates*, by which he intended to signify the two elements of music and thought in poetry. In this series appeared all his plays and poems until 1846, the year of his marriage. In *Bells and Pomegranates* No. III (1842) he printed the first of the poems in which he made a deliberate bid for wide popularity. No. VII, published in 1845, contains the first considerable body of poems for which Browning is still read with enjoyment, and which are in his most characteristic manner.[1] These were the *Dramatic Lyrics*,

[1] G. K. Chesterton (*Robert Browning*, 1904) called *Pippa Passes* 'the greatest poem ever written, with the exception of one or two by Walt Whitman, to express the sentiment of the pure love of humanity'. Of *Dramatic Lyrics* he wrote that they 'represent the arrival of the real Browning of literary history. . . . In *Dramatic Lyrics* he discovered the one thing that he could really do better than anyone else—the dramatic lyric. The form is absolutely original: he had discovered a new field of poetry, and in the centre of that field he had found himself.'

ELIZABETH BARRETT BROWNING IN 1859
From a chalk drawing by F. Talfourd

CLASPED HANDS OF ROBERT AND ELIZABETH BROWNING
From the bronze cast by Harriet Hosmer, 1853

as he called them, including *Pictor Ignotus*, *The Lost Leader*, *Home Thoughts from Abroad*, *The Bishop orders his Tomb in St. Praxed's Church*.

At this time, seeking unsuccessfully for poetic popularity, he was, less actively, seeking also for his ideal of womanhood, not an easy quest for one so bound emotionally to the mother he idealised. In 1844 he paid his second visit to Italy, and on his return in the winter he found waiting for him the two volumes of the collected poems of a successful poetess, Elizabeth Moulton Barrett. He read the poems through, almost breathless with admiration, and was delighted to find a flattering reference to himself. In Lady Geraldine's Courtship she speaks of reading

'. . . from Browning some "Pomegranate", which, if cut deep
   down the middle,
Shows a heart within blood-tinctured, of a veined humanity.'

He at once wrote to her the following letter:

'*New Cross, Hatcham, Surrey*.
(postmark Jan. 10, 1845)

'I love your verses with all my heart, dear Miss Barrett,—and this is no off-hand complimentary letter that I shall write,—whatever else, no prompt matter-of-course recognition of your genius, and there a graceful and natural end of the thing. Since the day last week when I first read your poems, I quite laughed to remember how I have been turning and turning again in my mind what I should be able to tell you of their effect upon me, for in the first flush of delight I thought I would this once get out of my habit of purely passive enjoyment, when I do really enjoy and thoroughly justify my admiration—perhaps even, as a loyal fellow-craftsman should, try and find fault and do you some little good to be proud of hereafter!—but nothing comes of it all—so into me has it gone, and part of me has it become, this great living poetry of yours, not a flower of which but took root and grew—Oh, how different that is from lying to be dried and pressed flat, and prized highly, and put in a book with a proper account at top and bottom, and shut up and put away . . . and the book called a "Flora", besides!

After all, I need not give up the thought of doing that, too, in time; because even now, talking with whoever is worthy, I can give a reason for my faith in one and another excellence, the fresh strange music, the affluent language, the exquisite pathos and true new brave thought; but in this addressing myself to you—your own self, and for the first time, my feeling rises altogether. I do, as I say, love these books with all my heart—and I love you too. Do you know I was once not very far from seeing—really seeing you? Mr. Kenyon said to me one morning "Would you like to see Miss Barrett?" then he went to announce me,—then he returned . . . you were too unwell, and now it is years ago, and I feel as at some untoward passage in my travels, as if I had been close, so close, to some world's-wonder in chapel or crypt, only a screen to push and I might have entered, but there was some slight, so it now seems, slight and just sufficient bar to admission, and the half-opened door shut, and I went home my thousands of miles, and the sight was never to be?

Well, these Poems were to be, and this true thankful joy and pride with which I feel myself,

'Yours ever faithfully,

'ROBERT BROWNING.'

Elizabeth replied, and before long they were exchanging letters on terms of the friendliest mutual admiration and approval. Browning begged to be allowed to visit her; she made many objections, but at last on May 20th, 1845, the two poets met for the first time.

III

MARRIAGE AND SUCCESS

The several close friends whom Browning had had among women had been, without exception, older than he. It was as if he were unconsciously seeking a substitute for his mother. Elizabeth Barrett was six years his senior. Born in 1806, the daughter of a West Indian merchant and slave-owner—a curious coincidence—she spent her early life in the heart of the country, at Hope End, near Ledbury in Herefordshire. She was an intellectual prodigy, and at thirteen she wrote an epic poem in four books on the subject of Marathon. At fifteen a spinal injury caused by a fall made her for several years an invalid. Although it afterwards proved to have been by no means the permanent injury that everyone supposed, it became the physical basis for a psychological invalidism from which in the end only Browning rescued her.

At twenty-two Elizabeth lost her mother; depending even more on the love of her father, she became his chief companion and household adviser.

In 1835 the family removed to London, as Mr. Barrett's business affairs required his daily attendance in the city. In 1838 they found a permanent home at No. 50 Wimpole Street, and Elizabeth was obliged to spend the winter at Torquay on account of her health. Her favourite brother, Edward, accompanied her. She liked the place so much that next year she persuaded Edward to stay on into the summer months. In July he went for a sail with friends and was drowned. Prostrate with grief and a sense of guilt as the cause of her brother's death, Elizabeth suffered a prolonged emotional crisis, and was not able to return to London until 1841. Here, surrounded by books and distracted by voluminous correspondence with her friends, she began her life as the poetess and recluse. She lay all day on her sofa in a hermetically sealed room in which the flowers sent by her friends speedily withered. In this she was obeying her doctors' instructions, which were in accordance with the medical practice of the day. Although her correspondence then, as at all times, was witty, gay and shrewd, she was profoundly unhappy. There was no possibility of escape from the prison of her own illness and inaction, and of the mingled love and dread by which she and her brothers and sisters were bound to their father. Absolute filial obedience was expected of his children as a sacred duty. Elizabeth was thirty-nine. Neither she nor any of the others had married. To marry and leave their father would be the basest act of treachery and disloyalty. Edward Moulton Barrett was a domestic tyrant, and it is easier to condemn than to defend him. His relations with Elizabeth, his favourite child, can only be understood, however, as arising as much from her need of him as from his demands on her.

Although in 1845 she regarded her life in the world as at an end, she kept up a lively interest in the intellectual movements of her time. The appearance of her collected poems in that year brought her letters of congratulation from people of fame and discernment, notably from Carlyle. The adverse criticisms of Browning's poems had aroused her feeling of chivalry for an unsuccessful and deserving poet. Her reference to him in her poems was the occasion of his first letter to her. From the beginning Browning seems to have recognised her, even before he saw her, as the woman for whom he had been looking so long in vain. He determined first to break in upon her seclusion and visit her; and then to woo and marry her.

It might be supposed that he acted from motives of chivalry. It was not so. Had it been, it is certain she would never have accepted him. On the contrary, he looked up to her, from motives of admiration and from his own need, not down to her, from pity. She was a famous, a great poet: her genius was something 'divine'. Upon that he always insisted, with absolute conviction. Her poetry is not now admired; it has suffered the fate of most poetry that enjoys wide popularity in its day. Not even the *Sonnets from the Portuguese*, addressed to Browning, have much more than an autobiographical interest, although they have been extravagantly praised. Browning wanted Elizabeth because he was weak, dependent, and without a sense of purpose. She wanted Browning for very similar reasons. Their relation has been called 'symbiotic'—that is, the life of each was incomplete without the other. Browning needed a purpose in life: to restore Elizabeth to health, to rescue her from prison, and to marry her became the purpose of his life. It was the only part of his life as a man as distinct from his work as a poet, which had any significance, as he well knew. To liberate herself from the strongest and the oldest bonds of her existence, dependence on her father and her ill-health, and answer her lover's need—this became Elizabeth's purpose in life.

Browning persuaded her first to get up from her sofa, and then to open her door and windows, and go out into the air.[1] Very early in their correspondence he seems to have made some rash and clumsy attempt at a proposal of marriage, for which she rebuked him. He withdrew incontinently and asked for his letter back, so that he might burn it. Later, she asked for the letter again, but it had been destroyed. The progress of their courtship can be read in the numerous surviving letters. By far the better of the two as a poet, Browning was a poor letter writer; her letters, by contrast, are full of life, gaiety, and fun.[2]

By January 1846, a year after his first letter, Browning had renewed his proposal of marriage, and almost imperceptibly she had accepted it. But she could not bring herself to tear away the bonds of filial obedience. It was agreed that they should marry and escape to Italy. Browning had no money, but Elizabeth's independent fortune was enough for both.

[1] That Elizabeth Barrett came to regard her captivity as in some way symptomatic of the social evils of her age is indicated by her reply to Thackeray who, as editor of *The Cornhill*, rejected her poem *Lord Walter's Wife* on the ground that his readers would resent its treatment of 'unlawful passion'. 'From your "Cornhill" standpoint (paterfamilias looking on)', she wrote, 'you are probably right ten times over. . . . But I am deeply convinced that the corruption of our society requires not shut doors and windows, but light and air.'

[2] One brief example of her style of letter writing must suffice. During one of the Brownings' visits to England they entertained the Poet Laureate. In a letter to a friend she commented: 'He dined with us, smoked with us, opened his heart to us (and the second bottle of port) and ended by reading *Maud* through from end to end, and going away at half-past two in the morning. If I had had a heart to spare, certainly he would have won mine. He is captivating with his frankness, confidingness, and unexampled *naïveté*! Think of his stopping in *Maud* every now and then—"There's a wonderful touch! That's very tender. How beautiful that is!"'

Mr. Barrett became suspicious of the visits of 'the pomegranate man', as he somewhat contemptuously called the penniless poet. Finally, in an almost hysterical atmosphere of suspense and foreboding, on September 12th, 1846, Elizabeth met her lover secretly at church and was married to him; a week later, they left England for Italy.

In falling in love with Elizabeth Barrett, in rescuing her from illness, despair, and the tyranny of a monomaniac father, in giving her fifteen years of happy married life, Browning achieved the most—and in a sense the only—significant act of his life. The courtship and elopement which was the sensation of the literary world at the time, and has ever since been regarded as one of the most delightful and satisfactory love stories of which so much detail is known, might have ended in tragedy. Knowing of the fifteen years of happiness, we are apt to forget this, and underrate the courage and enterprise of both the lovers—especially of Robert, since if Elizabeth had died as a result of the strain and excitement of leaving her home, he would never have been forgiven either by himself or by society. He was, as Chesterton expressed it, 'a thoroughly conventional man'; he was, by temperament and upbringing, respectable, and his respectability amounted to a passion. The marriage with Elizabeth was, in all the circumstances, an act of great daring; and its success must have had something to do with the optimistic outlook for which Browning became famous.

Their married life was spent mostly in Italy, especially at the Casa Guidi in Florence. Several attempts at reconciliation with Edward Moulton Barrett failed: to Elizabeth's lasting grief, he never opened one of her letters to him. There were differences between husband and wife, over three matters especially. One of these differences arose over certain of Elizabeth's political opinions; another source of dissatisfaction to Robert was the upbringing of their only son Pen, whom Elizabeth spoiled almost irretrievably; by the unwritten terms of their compact, Browning could not interfere. In marrying her, he had desired only to live by her will; it was she who must make the decisions. She had from the start striven against this,[1] but he had forced it on her.

The third subject of difference was Elizabeth's interest in the fashionable pastime of mesmerism, as it was called—that is, the investigation of spiritualistic phenomena. Browning disliked spiritualism because he considered that its practitioners were frauds, and because it threatened his wife's mental stability. Despite these differences, however, their life together was a happy one, not because it was from first to last idyllic, but because to both it was the only possible fulfilment of their personality and of what their two lives had been so far: to Elizabeth it was life itself, to Robert it was a motive for life; Elizabeth was the 'fixed foot' that gave his wandering spirit centre and equilibrium.

Browning was one of the least envious of men. He had loved Elizabeth from the start for her genius as a poet, since she seemed to be all that he was not. It is worth quoting in full two passages from his letters, since they reveal his view of his own work up to the time when the two poets met. On January 13th, 1845, he wrote to her:

'Your poetry must be, cannot but be, infinitely more to me than mine to you—for you *do* what I always wanted, hoped to do, and only seem now likely to do for the first time. You speak out, *you*,—I only make men and woman speak—give you truth broken into prismatic hues, and fear the pure white light, even if it is in me, but I am going to try.'

Again in February 1845:

'What I have printed gives *no* knowledge of me—it evidences abilities of various kinds, if you will—and a dramatic sympathy with certain modifications of passion . . . *that* I think—But I never

[1] On September 15th, 1846, she had written to him: 'In your ways towards me, you have acted throughout too much "the woman's part", as that is considered. You loved me because I was lower than others, that you might be generous and raise me up: —very characteristic for a woman (in her ideal standard) but quite wrong for a man, as again and again I used to signify to you, Robert—but you went on and did it all the same.'

have begun, even, what I hope I was born to begin and end—
"R.B. a poem"—and next, if I speak (and, God knows, feel) as if
what you have read were sadly imperfect demonstrations of even
mere ability, it is from no absurd vanity, though it might seem so—
these scenes and song-scraps *are* such mere and very escapes of my
inner power, which lives in me like the light in those crazy Medi-
terranean phares I have watched at sea, wherein the light is ever
revolving in a dark gallery, bright and alive, and only after a weary
interval leaps out, for a moment from the one narrow chink, and
then goes on with the blind wall between it and you. . . .'

It mattered little to Browning that his own poetic genius was
unrecognised, so long as Elizabeth continued to gain in fame
and popularity. When Wordsworth died in 1850 *The Athenæum*
proposed Elizabeth for the vacant place of Poet Laureate. No
one suggested Browning, and the honour fell to Tennyson. In
literary circles in Italy, and to their numerous visitors, Browning
was the husband of the poetess. Her *Aurora Leigh* went
into several editions rapidly, while Browning's *Men and
Women* (1855) failed of both popularity and the esteem of the
critics.

To say, as Osbert Burdett says, that the years of Browning's
marriage were 'not specially productive' is incomprehensible,
though it must be admitted that after *Men and Women* he under-
went a period of sterility. On present estimates of his work, he
wrote the best of it during the first ten years of his life with
Elizabeth. Many of his finest poems are included in *Men and
Women*. Elizabeth died in Italy in 1861, and in more ways than
one Browning never recovered from his loss. His critics have
at various times differed radically as to what his masterpiece
was. Some have proclaimed it to be *The Ring and the Book*, the
magnum opus with which Browning occupied himself after her
death. It consists of 20,000 lines, in which the same story is told
ten times. At present it appears to be an unread masterpiece.
Prolific he undoubtedly was during the remaining twenty-eight
years of his life, but in spite of occasional successes a modern

reader is likely to detect in his last phase a general lack of inspiration, a growing repetitiveness and verbosity, a love of the eccentric and grotesque as a substitute for the abounding felicity of much of the poetry from the *Dramatic Lyrics* to *Men and Women*.

After Elizabeth's death Browning returned to England, where he busied himself with his son's education. Except for regular visits to the Continent, he lived in London, gradually becoming a literary lion and, at last, one of the most esteemed poets of his time.

In 1864 he published *Dramatis Personæ*, and in 1867 a new collected edition of his poems; in 1868 the appearance of *The Ring and the Book* brought him fame and an assured position.[1]

He was fifty-six, and at that age a man who has devoted his life to poetry and published a considerable volume of work without achieving the popularity he has striven for, may fairly harvest the rewards of his labour. Then began the period of the honorary degrees at Oxford and Cambridge, the academic honours in Scotland, the eulogiums, the foundation of the Browning Society.[2] In a sense it was the dead poet who was being honoured. Reading his poems impartially to-day, we must feel that the genuine poet had died, even before his wife, only to revive fitfully in some of the slighter works of the later years. Society has rarely had much use for a living poet, and it was the man of ideas, the optimist, the rallying-point against

[1] *The Edinburgh Review* said: 'We must record at once our conviction, not merely that *The Ring and the Book* is beyond all parallel the supremest poetical achievement of our time, but that it is the most precious and profound spiritual treasure that England has produced since the days of Shakespeare.'

[2] 'With the greatest goodwill in the world Browning submitted himself to lionisation: a happy acquiescence which discovered him, on one occasion, drinking tea and eating muffins with female members of the Browning society at Newnham, who, having presented him with a wreath of roses, grouped themselves picturesquely at his feet, while the ageing poet sat "bland and ruddy and slightly buttery from the muffins, with the crown of pink roses laid upon his white locks, and looking like a lamb decked for sacrifice".' Betty Miller: *Robert Browning, A Portrait* (1952).

the pessimistic implications of Darwinism, that the later Victorians valued. 'The longer I live,' wrote Thomas Hardy in 1899, 'the more does Browning's character seem *the* literary puzzle of the nineteenth century. How could smug Christian optimism worthy of a dissenting grocer find a place inside a man who was so vast a seer and feeler when on neutral ground?' According to the analysis of Mrs. Betty Miller, Browning effected a schism between the poet and the man of society; inspiration was extinguished, and to this we owe the energetic but uninspired writing of the later years. Henry James confessed that he could never meet the real Browning, the poet: 'One man is the genius,' he said, 'the other's the bourgeois, and it's only the bourgeois whom we personally know.'

It was almost as if Browning had become one of his own *dramatis personæ*—a debonair, successful man, more like a banker than a poet, loquacious, loud-voiced, and a little self-satisfied. What inner disturbances went on behind the mask we shall never know for certain. It is doubtful whether the 'R. B.' which the world knew in the later Browning was exactly the 'R. B.— a poem' which he had projected for himself in the first letter to Elizabeth Barrett. Outwardly, at least, his old age was tranquil and contented. He was active to the last. When he died of heart-failure at the age of seventy-seven in his son's house at Venice, his last book of poems, *Asolando*, appeared fittingly on the day of his death.

The last poem in that volume, entitled *Epilogue*, speaks of life as a 'fight' and 'a march'; it may be that one clue to Browning's character lies in this lifelong preoccupation with the idea of fighting. The *Epilogue* to *Asolando* reads like the epitaph on a man of action. Possibly, like so many others, he thought of himself as essentially a man of action, but destined by temperament and aptitude to follow the 'sedentary trade' of writing. His repeated efforts in the field of drama and his many dramatic monologues based upon violent and sometimes melodramatic actions were in part a compensation for the inaction of his own life. *Childe Roland to the Dark Tower Came*, the strangest of his poems as well as one of the most powerful, is overcast by the sense of a frustrated desire for action in an ugly and malevolent world where all action seems futile and abortive. Nevertheless, as we have seen, only one significant act broke the outwardly uneventful course of his long life and coloured the whole of his subsequent thinking. For a deeper knowledge of Browning we must go to the poems.

IV

THE POETRY OF BROWNING

A detailed commentary on the poems in this selection is given in the Notes. It remains to add a general critical account which will help towards the understanding of Browning's poetry as a whole.

The most obvious thing about it is its volume: Browning lived a full poetic life, unhampered by material wants; we may be sure that anything he wanted to write he wrote; nothing he could achieve was frustrated by accidental happenings. With other poets, ill-health, the necessity to write for money, or the pressure of external circumstances hindered the free play of their genius, or gave it a stimulus it might otherwise have lacked. Browning had immense creative energy, uninhibited by psychological or social causes, though directed to some extent by the nature of Victorian susceptibilities, of which his own intense conventionalism made him continually aware. A non-conformist in religion, he was conformist in matters of social decorum.

Whatever its limitations, the Victorian reading public was one which read poetry, and consequently considered it had a right to determine what poets wrote. Browning wanted fame, and even popularity. He experimented ceaselessly; he was an inveterate improviser. He had, for instance, a working knowledge of keyboard music, and one of his pastimes was to go into a church and extemporise at the organ. It was as if his creative energy needed other outlets than poetry, immense as was his output in that field. His main fault of style is what we should expect from such an artist: he was careless of technical perfection, impatient of correction. His 'obscurity' is often simply carelessness: such lines as

> 'and, since beneath my roof
> Housed she who made home heaven, in heaven's behoof'
> (*A Forgiveness*)

are simply clumsy, though this sort of thing has been admired in Browning because of what some readers have taken to be a kind of homespun roughness. There is often a roughness in Donne's style, but it derives from internal emotional pressure and the deliberate wish to shock into attentiveness a public lulled by Spenserian mellifluence. It is difficult to find similar justification for Browning's frequent *gaucherie*; one may say that he was writing in protest against Tennysonian sweetness, but too often he writes roughly when he has nothing special to draw his readers' attention to. His inversions and tortuosities of syntax can too often be ascribed only to an unwillingness to revise. Of the virtues of the extemporising style we shall have something to say shortly.

Next to the volume of Browning's poetry we shall notice its variety. He wrote with equal facility short lyrics and long dramatic monologues. His short lyrics are not his best work, but some of them, such as *Meeting at Night* and *Misconceptions*, are memorable. So too are some of the brief utterances of tender regret and fleeting passion contained in his last volume, *Asolando*. The too-well-known lyric from *Pippa Passes*, with which this selection begins, is a rare expression of spontaneous happiness, objectionable only to those who imagine that poetry must always be sad, or who find in it the expression of a considered philosophy of life. 'All's right with the world' is no less true, taken out of its context, than many of the statements of poetry.

Nevertheless, the Browning of these brief lyrics is not the real Browning. Much nearer to that elusive spirit is the writer of the group of poems dealing with the psychology of love. *A Woman's Last Word*, *The Last Ride Together*, *Love Among the Ruins*, and *Two in the Campagna* are not only good in themselves, they are highly characteristic. They deal, not with the rapture, the surprise, the pain of youthful and spontaneous passion, but with the less easily apprehended and less obviously poetic theme of mature, adult love. Browning is one of the few poets who can dwell interestingly and feelingly on the kind of passion which is tempered by affection, the kind of love in which mutual respect and admiration exist between two intellectual equals. He alone can write of domestic love with ardour and without complacency. *By the Fireside* is an essential poem for the understanding of the real Browning. In it he expresses, more simply and movingly than anywhere else, the central core of his belief, the essential discovery he had lived to make.

> 'I am named and known by that moment's feat;
>   There took my station and degree;
> So grew my own small life complete,
>   As nature obtained her best of me—
> One born to love you, sweet!
>
> 'And to watch you sink by the fire-side now
>   Back again, as you mutely sit
> Musing by firelight, that great brow
>   And the spirit-small hand propping it,
> Yonder, my heart knows how!'

But though love was both centre and summit of Browning's life, it was not the whole. The greatest part of the creative energy which he discovered in himself long before he discovered Elizabeth, and which lasted long after he lost her, was taken up by the inexhaustible problems of the artist's life. What is the nature of art and the artist? What is their relation to the world and society? What should be their concern with ethics and religion? These questions were continuously present in his mind, and find their way again and again into his poems. *Popularity, Memorabilia, Home, 'Transcendentalism'* — these are some of the poems in which he deals with this theme, or group of themes. One of the most striking is *A Grammarian's Funeral*, by many considered to be among his finest work. Here for once the roughness of the style, its deliberate knottiness, is matched with the subject.

One of the themes which occupied Browning's thoughts throughout his life was that of natural instinct opposed to the corrupting influence of worldly conventions. As an early follower of Shelley, Browning believed in the natural instincts and in natural goodness. We have seen how his own conventionality and a desire for success as poet drove him to disguise this preoccupation. Of the central and greatest period of Browning's poetry an American critic has written:

'Through his dramatic experiments Browning had learned to project his insights outward and to give them objective embodiment in imaginary characterizations. Henceforth he would drop the pretence of external action and confine his attention to the portrayal of individuals under the stress of such interior, psychological conflicts as characterize the play of his own complex and boldly original mind. Seemingly so remote from their creator in time and place and circumstance, these figures would thus become Browning's agents for delivering to his age the messages which he had failed to get across in other ways.'[1]

One of the best of the dramatic monologues, *My Last Duchess*, was written as early as 1842. In it Browning perfected the

[1] E. D. H. Johnson, *The Alien Vision of Victorian Poetry* (Princeton University Press, 1952).

technique which he was to use in most of his important later poems. It is good partly because it is short—it contains nothing superfluous; and partly because it is perfectly objective—it contains no moralising; the reader is left to extract the meaning for himself; moreover, the language and imagery are clear, vivid, and telling. It is in every way a masterly poem. The theme is that of natural goodness and sweetness of character wantonly destroyed by the ruthlessness of a proud and cynical worldling. *Fra Lippo Lippi* is a more elaborate self-portrait of an artist constrained to break the bonds of rigid monasticism in order that his natural instincts as a man **may** have free play; otherwise he cannot fulfil himself as an artist. *A Toccata of Galuppi's*, in an altogether lighter manner, makes a similar plea for freedom in self-expression, even for the frivolous worldlings of a decayed and useless society.

The Bishop orders his Tomb in St. Praxed's Church is a penetrating exposure of vain and cynical materialism in high places. *Andrea del Sarto* is the condemnation of a man who fails to make the most of his gifts. It presents a fine contrast to *A Grammarian's Funeral*. But, as has often been noticed, it was not in Browning's real nature to condemn unconditionally. Indeed, forgiveness is another of the recurrent themes of his poetry. The comparatively early *A Lost Leader* concludes on a note of forgiveness, and the idea is more fully treated in *Sibrandus Schafnaburgensis*. To Browning, life presented a complex pattern of motives and influences, and he was concerned not only to portray men and women but to understand them; often he discovered that in understanding he could forgive. He has been compared earlier with Meredith. The comparison has again been made in a recent article already quoted: 'Meredith exposes Sir Willoughby Patterne and condemns him in the process: Browning exposes Sludge and vindicates him. Such benevolence is at the bottom of Browning's view of life.'[1] The same idea was expressed by G. K. Chesterton

[1] J. A. Boulton, see footnote, p. viii.

so memorably and characteristically that his words are worth quoting in full:

> 'In all his life, it must constantly be remembered, he tried always the most difficult things. Just as he tried the queerest metres and attempted to manage them, so he tried the queerest human souls and attempted to stand in their place. Charity was his basic philosophy; but it was, as it were, a fierce charity, a charity that went man-hunting. He was a kind of cosmic detective who walked into the foulest of thieves' kitchens and accused men publicly of virtue.'

Chesterton was also thinking especially of the monologue *Mr. Sludge the Medium*, which, based on the American mesmerist David Home, embodied all Browning's hatred of the charlatan who had so impressed Elizabeth. Interesting though the poem is psychologically, it is a good example of Browning's method gone to seed. For the digressions and repetitions, as well as the flatness of the verse, despite occasional interludes of hysterical melodrama, make it almost unendurably tedious. To include it, the present selection would have had to be much fuller.

Much of the discussion of Browning's poems which goes on periodically is concerned with this question of their length. Osbert Burdett, for instance, wrote:

> 'Unfortunately, for many readers the vividness is defeated by the length. You have to attend, perhaps to think, the whole time, and very few are prepared to pay so stiff a price for poetry. It is the length and the amount of discussion that deprives Browning of many readers, and, as neither quality can be explained away, it is impossible to alter this.'[1]

Only Browning, one might add, could have written a poem of two hundred lines and called it *One Word More*. Burdett, however, was writing in 1928, when long poems were almost entirely out of fashion and brevity was regarded as a virtue. To-day we have more patience with the long poem; and Browning's bulk, which is after all a sign of creative energy, is coming to be looked on more favourably. An anonymous reviewer in *The Times*

[1] See footnote, p. [xi].

Literary Supplement for June 4th, 1954, says, for instance: 'Part of the greatness of Browning, as of all the Victorians, does lie, of course, in his huge uneven energy, his mere bulk.'

But length in poetry is not altogether a matter of fashion, nor of individual taste. Unless a poem has very strict organic unity, and is free from digressions and repetition, we cannot easily retain in our minds an impression of it as a whole. *The Ancient Mariner* possesses such unity. Most of Browning's long poems do not. Moreover, we can find poetry not merely in the whole course and structure of Coleridge's poem, but also in its details, its countless memorable phrases. We are entitled to look for poetry in detail when judging of a poet's work. There are many tedious and flat pages in Browning. There are also many verse portraits and narratives which win our approval as a whole without arousing our admiration in any particulars. Can we find the other sort of poetry in Browning?

Enough has been said about his themes and subjects to suggest that he was a poet on a big scale. There is wealth and variety in his work, and there are many poems of which space has not here allowed of so much as a mention which will repay discovery and study. Poetry there is, certainly, in themes and ideas; but unless there is poetry also in details and particulars, we are perhaps justified in denying the highest place to its author. In short, we are inclined to value a poet as much for his style as for the general design of his work—more, some would say. It remains to say something of Browning's style.

He improvised, and he experimented. His syntax is often clumsy. His verse sometimes shows the faults of his prose—a looseness of structure betrayed in his fondness for dashes instead of other punctuation-marks, an inability to speak gracefully and lucidly. His curious rhyming habits have been well commented on by Chesterton:

> 'But the rhyming frenzy of Browning has no particular relation
> even to the poems in which it occurs. It is not a dance to any
> measure; it can only be called the horse-play of literature. It may

be noted, for example, as a rather curious fact, that the ingenious rhymes are generally only mathematical triumphs, not triumphs of any kind of assonance.'

It is strange, in view of some of the claims that have been made for Browning, that he is not much quoted for his poetry—where he has been most often quoted it is for his thought; those who look for moral maxims and ethical epigrams have found plenty to quote in Browning; but he is not rich in the kind of felicities that are quoted and re-quoted from Shakespeare, and Donne, and Keats. Nevertheless, at his best Browning has ample felicity of style, grace in diction, vividness in imagery, charm in atmosphere. Which are the poems that come nearest to perfection, that are characteristic and unique, that reveal—in short—the real Browning? With some hesitation, I would be inclined to vote for those poems where a certain lightness of touch is combined with an easy, colloquial style—a diction precise but not pedantic, a movement free yet not irregular. Some of these are: *A Toccata of Galuppi's*, *The Englishman in Italy*, '*De Gustibus——*', *How It Strikes a Contemporary*, *Youth and Art*, *Up at a Villa—Down in the City*. Admittedly the Browning of these poems seems of smaller stature than the Browning of *Andrea del Sarto*, *The Bishop Orders His Tomb*, and *Fra Lippo Lippi*. But in any case, something of the qualities I have mentioned is to be found among these latter poems, especially *The Bishop Orders His Tomb*, which I would place high on the list. The poems I have named do not for the most part tell stories; still less do they moralise or philosophise; they do not display spiritual agony or metaphysical doubt; they are not passionate; nor are they melodramatic, or forced, or pretentious. Some readers may prefer Browning's grander failures; to me these are his less grand but more assured successes. They are happy poems, light-hearted, but not without a certain wistful melancholy. They reveal his love of the real world, the warm sensuous world of the Mediterranean; the things they describe can be seen, felt, touched, tasted, even smelt. They are very good of their kind, and it is a kind none too common in English poetry. Critics have at various times acclaimed *The Ring and the Book*, or *Porphyria's Lover*, or *Childe Roland* as Browning's 'masterpiece'. This lack of general agreement, sixty years after his death, about which *are* his greatest poems, may be an indication that he wrote no poems of the highest quality, and that more has been claimed for him than he deserves. I do not think, however, that he is a poet of a single 'masterpiece'. There are many Brownings, and each reader will choose his favourite. Some may prefer the seer; some the preacher; some the novelist, the psychologist, the teacher. Some have been attracted to the portrayer of the grotesque in nature and humanity. But if we are looking for Browning the poet, the maker of memorable speech in rhyme and rhythm, we must look among the poems I have named, and others like them. Browning believed, at heart, not that 'All's right with the world', but at any rate that the world was good. He was at his best when he recorded the world's goodness, as proved upon his own pulses, not when he moralised or preached about it. To conclude with a reference to his early idol: there is an element of truth in Shelley's idealised statement about poetry—'Poetry is the record of the best and happiest moments of the happiest and best minds.' Much of the happiness, for a poet, comes from the recording of those moments. The moments when he was improvising, in his own personal idiom and manner, on the worth and beauty of the world of which his senses brought him abundant daily evidence—these were the best moments in the life of Robert Browning, poet.   J. R.

Chalfont St Giles,
  July, 1954

SELECTED POEMS

Pippa's Song

The year's at the spring
And day's at the morn;
Morning's at seven;
The hill-side's dew-pearled;
The lark's on the wing;
The snail's on the thorn:
God's in his heaven—
All's right with the world!

My Last Duchess

Ferrara

That's my last Duchess painted on the wall,
Looking as if she were alive. I call
That piece a wonder, now: Frà Pandolf's hands
Worked busily a day, and there she stands.
Will't please you sit and look at her? I said
'Frà Pandolf' by design, for never read
Strangers like you that pictured countenance,
The depth and passion of its earnest glance,
But to myself they turned (since none puts by
The curtain I have drawn for you, but I)   10
And seemed as they would ask me, if they durst,
How such a glance came there; so, not the first
Are you to turn and ask thus. Sir, 'twas not
Her husband's presence only, called that spot

I

Of joy into the Duchess' cheek: perhaps
Frà Pandolf chanced to say 'Her mantle laps
'Over my lady's wrist too much,' or 'Paint
'Must never hope to reproduce the faint
'Half-flush that dies along her throat' such stuff
Was courtesy, she thought, and cause enough   20
For calling up that spot of joy. She had
A heart—how shall I say?—too soon made glad,
Too easily impressed; she liked whate'er
She looked on, and her looks went everywhere.
Sir, 'twas all one! My favour at her breast,
The dropping of the daylight in the West,
The bough of cherries some officious fool
Broke in the orchard for her, the white mule
She rode with round the terrace—all and each
Would draw from her alike the approving speech,   30
Or blush, at least. She thanked men,—good! but thanked
Somehow—I know not how—as if she ranked
My gift of a nine-hundred-years-old name
With anybody's gift. Who'd stoop to blame
This sort of trifling? Even had you skill
In speech—(which I have not)—to make your will
Quite clear to such an one, and say, 'Just this
'Or that in you disgusts me; here you miss,
'Or there exceed the mark'—and if she let
Herself be lessoned so, nor plainly set   40
Her wits to yours, forsooth, and made excuse,
—E'en then would be some stooping; and I choose
Never to stoop. Oh sir, she smiled, no doubt,
Whene'er I passed her; but who passed without
Much the same smile? This grew; I gave commands;
Then all smiles stopped together. There she stands
As if alive. Will't please you rise? We'll meet
The company below, then. I repeat,
The Count your master's known munificence

Is ample warrant that no just pretence
Of mine for dowry will be disallowed;
Though his fair daughter's self, as I avowed
At starting, is my object. Nay, we'll go
Together down, sir. Notice Neptune, though,
Taming a sea-horse, thought a rarity,
Which Claus of Innsbruck cast in bronze for me

Sibrandus Schafnaburgensis

1

Plague take all your pedants, say I!
   He who wrote what I hold in my hand,
Centuries back was so good as to die,
   Leaving this rubbish to cumber the land;
This, that was a book in its time,
   Printed on paper and bound in leather,
Last month in the white of a matin-prime
   Just when the birds sang all together.

2

Into the garden I brought it to read,
   And under the arbute and laurustine
Read it, so help me grace in my need,
   From title-page to closing line.
Chapter on chapter did I count,
   As a curious traveller counts Stonehenge;
Added up the mortal amount;
   And then proceeded to my revenge.

3

3

Yonder's a plum-tree with a crevice
   An owl would build in, were he but sage;
For a lap of moss, like a fine pont-levis
   In a castle of the Middle Age,
Joins to a lip of gum, pure amber;
   When he'd be private, there might he spend
Hours alone in his lady's chamber:
   Into this crevice I dropped our friend.

4

Splash, went he, as under he ducked,
   —At the bottom, I knew, rain-drippings stagnate:
Next, a handful of blossoms I plucked
   To bury him with, my bookshelf's magnate;
Then I went in-doors, brought out a loaf,
   Half a cheese, and a bottle of Chablis;
Lay on the grass and forgot the oaf
   Over a jolly chapter of Rabelais.

5

Now, this morning, betwixt the moss
   And gum that locked our friend in limbo,
A spider had spun his web across,
   And sat in the midst with arms akimbo:
So, I took pity, for learning's sake,
   And, *de profundis, accentibus lætis,*
Cantate! quoth I, as I got a rake;
   And up I fished his delectable treatise.

6

Here you have it, dry in the sun,
    With all the binding all of a blister,
And great blue spots where the ink has run,
    And reddish streaks that wink and glister
O'er the page so beautifully yellow:
    Oh, well have the droppings played their tricks!
Did he guess how toadstools grow, this fellow?
    Here's one stuck in his chapter six!

7

How did he like it when the live creatures
    Tickled and toused and browsed him all over,
And worm, slug, eft, with serious features,
    Came in, each one, for his right of trover?
—When the water-beetle with great blind deaf face
    Made of her eggs the stately deposit,
And the newt borrowed just so much of the preface
    As tiled in the top of his black wife's closet?

8

All that life and fun and romping,
    All that frisking and twisting and coupling,
While slowly our poor friend's leaves were swamping
    And clasps were cracking and covers suppling!
As if you had carried sour John Knox
    To the play-house at Paris, Vienna or Munich,
Fastened him into a front-row box,
    And danced off the ballet with trousers and tunic.

Come, old martyr! What, torment enough is it?
  Back to my room shall you take your sweet self.
Good-bye, mother-beetle; husband-eft, *sufficit!*
  See the snug niche I have made on my shelf!
A.'s book shall prop you up, B.'s shall cover you,
  Here's C. to be grave with, or D. to be gay,
And with E. on each side, and F. right over you,
  Dry-rot at ease till the Judgment-day!

The Lost Leader

Just for a handful of silver he left us,
  Just for a riband to stick in his coat—
Found the one gift of which fortune bereft us,
  Lost all the others she lets us devote;
They, with the gold to give, doled him out silver,
  So much was theirs who so little allowed:
How all our copper had gone for his service!
  Rags—were they purple, his heart had been proud!
We that had loved him so, followed him, honoured him,
  Lived in his mild and magnificent eye,
Learned his great language, caught his clear accents,
  Made him our pattern to live and to die!
Shakespeare was of us, Milton was for us,
  Burns, Shelley, were with us,—they watch from their graves!
He alone breaks from the van and the freemen,
  —He alone sinks to the rear and the slaves!

We shall march prospering,—not thro' his presence;
  Songs may inspirit us,—not from his lyre;
Deeds will be done,—while he boasts his quiescence,
  Still bidding crouch whom the rest bade aspire:

Blot out his name, then, record one lost soul more,
   One task more declined, one more footpath untrod,
One more devils'-triumph and sorrow for angels,
   One wrong more to man, one more insult to God!
Life's night begins: let him never come back to us!
   There would be doubt, hesitation and pain,
Forced praise on our part—the glimmer of twilight,
   Never glad confident morning again!
Best fight on well, for we taught him—strike gallantly,
   Menace our heart ere we master his own;
Then let him receive the new knowledge and wait us,
   Pardoned in heaven, the first by the throne!

The Lost Mistress

All's over, then: does truth sound bitter
   As one at first believes?
Hark, 'tis the sparrows' good-night twitter
   About your cottage eaves!

And the leaf-buds on the vine are woolly,
   I noticed that, to-day;
One day more bursts them open fully
   —You know the red turns grey.

To-morrow we meet the same then, dearest?
   May I take your hand in mine?
Mere friends are we,—well, friends the merest
   Keep much that I resign:

For each glance of the eye so bright and black,
    Though I keep with heart's endeavour,—
Your voice, when you wish the snowdrops back,
    Though it stay in my soul for ever!—

Yet I will but say what mere friends say,
    Or only a thought stronger;
I will hold your hand but as long as all may,
    Or so very little longer!

Meeting at Night

The grey sea and the long black land;
And the yellow half-moon large and low;
And the startled little waves that leap
In fiery ringlets from their sleep,
As I gain the cove with pushing prow,
And quench its speed i' the slushy sand.

Then a mile of warm sea-scented beach;
Three fields to cross till a farm appears;
A tap at the pane, the quick sharp scratch
And blue spurt of a lighted match,
And a voice less loud, thro' its joys and fears,
Than the two hearts beating each to each!

Parting at Morning

Round the cape of a sudden came the sea,
And the sun looked over the mountain's rim:
And straight was a path of gold for him,
And the need of a world of men for me.

Song

Nay but you, who do not love her,
   Is she not pure gold, my mistress?
Holds earth aught—speak truth—above her?
   Aught like this tress, see, and this tress,
And this last fairest tress of all,
So fair, see, ere I let it fall?

Because, you spend your lives in praising;
   To praise, you search the wide world over:
Then why not witness, calmly gazing,
   If earth holds aught—speak truth—above her?
Above this tress, and this, I touch
But cannot praise, I love so much!

Home-Thoughts, from Abroad

Oh, to be in England
Now that April's there,
And whoever wakes in England
Sees, some morning, unaware,
That the lowest boughs and the brushwood sheaf
Round the elm-tree bole are in tiny leaf,
While the chaffinch sings on the orchard bough
In England—now!

And after April, when May follows,
And the whitethroat builds, and all the swallows!
Hark, where my blossomed pear-tree in the hedge
Leans to the field and scatters on the clover
Blossoms and dewdrops—at the bent spray s edge—
That's the wise thrush; he sings each song twice over,
Lest you should think he never could recapture
The first fine careless rapture!
And though the fields look rough with hoary dew,
All will be gay when noontide wakes anew
The buttercups, the little children's dower
—Far brighter than this gaudy melon-flower!

Home-Thoughts, *from the Sea*

Nobly, nobly Cape Saint Vincent to the North-west died away;
Sunset ran, one glorious blood-red, reeking into Cadiz Bay;
Bluish 'mid the burning water, full in face Trafalgar lay;
In the dimmest North-east distance dawned Gibraltar grand
    and gray;
'Here and here did England help me: how can I help England?'—
    say,
Whoso turns as I, this evening, turn to God to praise and pray,
While Jove's planet rises yonder, silent over Africa.

The Englishman in Italy

Piano di Sorrento

Fortù, Fortù, my beloved one,
    Sit here by my side,
On my knees put up both little feet!
    I was sure, if I tried,
I could make you laugh spite of Sirocco.
    Now, open your eyes,
Let me keep you amused till he vanish
    In black from the skies,
With telling my memories over
    As you tell your beads;   10
All the Plain saw me gather, I garland
    —The flowers or the weeds.

Time for rain! for your long hot dry Autumn
    Had net-worked with brown
The white skin of each grape on the bunches,
    Marked like a quail's crown,
Those creatures you make such account of,
    Whose heads,—speckled white
Over brown like a great spider's back,
    As I told you last night,—   20
Your mother bites off for her supper.
    Red-ripe as could be,
Pomegranates were chapping and splitting
    In halves on the tree:
And betwixt the loose walls of great flintstone,
    Or in the thick dust

On the path, or straight out of the rock-side,
    Wherever could thrust
Some burnt sprig of bold hardy rock-flower
    Its yellow face up,   30
For the prize were great butterflies fighting,
    Some five for one cup.
So, I guessed, ere I got up this morning,
    What change was in store,
By the quick rustle-down of the quail-nets
    Which woke me before
I could open my shutter, made fast
    With a bough and a stone,
And look thro' the twisted dead vine-twigs,
    Sole lattice that's known.   40
Quick and sharp rang the rings down the net-poles,
    While, busy beneath,
Your priest and his brother tugged at them,
    The rain in their teeth.
And out upon all the flat house-roofs
    Where split figs lay drying,
The girls took the frails under cover:
    Nor use seemed in trying
To get out the boats and go fishing,
    For, under the cliff,   50
Fierce the black water frothed o'er the blind-rock.
    No seeing our skiff
Arrive about noon from Amalfi,
    —Our fisher arrive,
And pitch down his basket before us,
    All trembling alive
With pink and grey jellies, your sea-fruit;
    You touch the strange lumps,
And mouths gape there, eyes open, all manner
    Of horns and of humps,   60

Which only the fisher looks grave at,
    While round him like imps
Cling screaming the children as naked
    And brown as his shrimps;
Himself too as bare to the middle
    —You see round his neck
The string and its brass coin suspended,
    That saves him from wreck.
But to-day not a boat reached Salerno,
    So back, to a man,   70
Came our friends, with whose help in the vineyards
    Grape-harvest began.
In the vat, halfway up in our house-side,
    Like blood the juice spins,
While your brother all bare-legged is dancing
    Till breathless he grins
Dead-beaten in effort on effort
    To keep the grapes under,
Since still when he seems all but master,
    In pours the fresh plunder   80
From girls who keep coming and going
    With basket on shoulder,
And eyes shut against the rain's driving
    Your girls that are older,—
For under the hedges of aloe,
    And where, on its bed
Of the orchard's black mould, the love-apple
    Lies pulpy and red,
All the young ones are kneeling and filling
    Their laps with the snails   90
Tempted out by this first rainy weather,—
    Your best of regales,
As to-night will be proved to my sorrow,
    When, supping in state,

We shall feast our grape-gleaners (two dozen,
    Three over one plate)
With lasagne so tempting to swallow
    In slippery ropes,
And gourds fried in great purple slices,
    That colour of popes.   100
Meantime, see the grape bunch they've brought you:
    The rain-water slips
O'er the heavy blue bloom on each globe
    Which the wasp to your lips
Still follows with fretful persistence:
    Nay, taste, while awake,
This half of a curd-white smooth cheese-ball
    That peels, flake by flake,
Like an onion, each smoother and whiter;
    Next, sip this weak wine   110
From the thin green glass flask, with its stopper,
    A leaf of the vine;
And end with the prickly-pear's red flesh
    That leaves thro' its juice
The stony black seeds on your pearl-teeth.
    Sirocco is loose!
Hark, the quick, whistling pelt of the olives
    Which, thick in one's track,
Tempt the stranger to pick up and bite them,
    Tho' not yet half black!   120
How the old twisted olive trunks shudder,
    The medlars let fall
Their hard fruit, and the brittle great fig-trees
    Snap off, figs and all,
For here comes the whole of the tempest!
    No refuge, but creep
Back again to my side and my shoulder,
    And listen or sleep.

O how will your country show next week,
    When all the vine-boughs   130
Have been stripped of their foliage to pasture
    The mules and the cows?
Last eve, I rode over the mountains;
    Your brother, my guide,
Soon left me, to feast on the myrtles
    That offered, each side,
Their fruit-balls, black, glossy and luscious,—
    Or strip from the sorbs
A treasure, or, rosy and wondrous,
    Those hairy gold orbs!   140
But my mule picked his sure sober path out,
    Just stopping to neigh
When he recognized down in the valley
    His mates on their way
With the faggots and barrels of water;
    And soon we emerged
From the plain, where the woods could scarce follow;
    And still as we urged
Our way, the woods wondered, and left us,
    As up still we trudged   150
Though the wild path grew wilder each instant,
    And place was e'en grudged
'Mid the rock-chasms and piles of loose stones
    Like the loose broken teeth
Of some monster which climbed there to die
    From the ocean beneath—
Place was grudged to the silver-grey fume-weed
    That clung to the path,
And dark rosemary ever a-dying
    That, 'spite the wind's wrath,   160
So loves the salt rock's face to seaward,
    And lentisks as staunch

To the stone where they root and bear berries,
    And . . . what shows a branch
Coral-coloured, transparent, with circlets
    Of pale seagreen leaves;
Over all trod my mule with the caution
    Of gleaners o'er sheaves,
Still, foot after foot like a lady,
    Till, round after round,   170
He climbed to the top of Calvano,
    And God's own profound
Was above me, and round me the mountains,
    And under, the sea,
And within me my heart to bear witness
    What was and shall be.
Oh, heaven and the terrible crystal!
    No rampart excludes
Your eye from the life to be lived
    In the blue solitudes.   180
Oh, those mountains, their infinite movement!
    Still moving with you;
For, ever some new head and breast of them
    Thrusts into view
To observe the intruder; you see it
    If quickly you turn
And, before they escape you surprise them.
    They grudge you should learn
How the soft plains they look on, lean over
    And love (they pretend)   190
—Cower beneath them, the flat sea-pine crouches,
    The wild fruit-trees bend,
E'en the myrtle-leaves curl, shrink and shut:
    All is silent and grave:
'Tis a sensual and timorous beauty,
    How fair! but a slave.

So, I turned to the sea; and there slumbered
    As greenly as ever
Those isles of the siren, your Galli;
    No ages can sever   200
The Three, nor enable their sister
    To join them,—halfway
On the voyage, she looked at Ulysses—
    No farther to-day,
Tho' the small one, just launched in the wave,
    Watches breast-high and steady
From under the rock, her bold sister
    Swum halfway already.
Fortù, shall we sail there together
    And see from the sides   210
Quite new rocks show their faces, new haunts
    Where the siren abides?
Shall we sail round and round them, close over
    The rocks, tho' unseen,
That ruffle the grey glassy water
    To glorious green?
Then scramble from splinter to splinter,
    Reach land and explore,
On the largest, the strange square black turret
    With never a door,   220
Just a loop to admit the quick lizards;
    Then, stand there and hear
The birds' quiet singing, that tells us
    What life is, so clear?
—The secret they sang to Ulysses
    When, ages ago,
He heard and he knew this life's secret
    I hear and I know.

Ah, see! The sun breaks o'er Calvano;
    He strikes the great gloom   230

And flutters it o'er the mount's summit
　　　In airy gold fume.
All is over. Look out, see the gipsy,
　　　Our tinker and smith,
Has arrived, set up bellows and forge,
　　　And down-squatted forthwith
To his hammering, under the wall there;
　　　One eye keeps aloof
The urchins that itch to be putting
　　　His jews'-harps to proof,　　　　　　　240
While the other, thro' locks of curled wire,
　　　Is watching how sleek
Shines the hog, come to share in the windfall
　　　—Chew, abbot's own cheek!
All is over. Wake up and come out now,
　　　And down let us go,
And see the fine things got in order
　　　At church for the show
Of the Sacrament, set forth this evening.
　　　To-morrow's the Feast　　　　　　　250
Of the Rosary's Virgin, by no means
　　　Of Virgins the least,
As you'll hear in the off-hand discourse
　　　Which (all nature, no art)
The Dominican brother, these three weeks,
　　　Was getting by heart.
Not a pillar nor post but is dizened
　　　With red and blue papers;
All the roof waves with ribbons, each altar
　　　A-blaze with long tapers;　　　　　　260
But the great masterpiece is the scaffold
　　　Rigged glorious to hold
All the fiddlers and fifers and drummers
　　　And trumpeters bold,

Not afraid of Bellini nor Auber,
  Who, when the priest's hoarse,
Will strike us up something that's brisk
  For the feast's second course.
And then will the flaxen-wigged Image
  Be carried in pomp   270
Thro' the plain, while in gallant procession
  The priests mean to stomp.
All round the glad church lie old bottles
  With gunpowder stopped,
Which will be, when the Image re-enters,
  Religiously popped;
And at night from the crest of Calvano
  Great bonfires will hang,
On the plain will the trumpets join chorus,
  And more poppers bang.   280
At all events, come—to the garden
  As far as the wall;
See me tap with a hoe on the plaster
  Till out there shall fall
A scorpion with wide angry nippers!

  —'Such trifles!' you say?
Fortù, in my England at home,
  Men meet gravely to-day
And debate, if abolishing Corn-laws
  Be righteous and wise   290
—If 'twere proper, Sirocco should vanish
  In black from the skies!

The Bishop Orders His Tomb at Saint Praxed's Church

Rome, 15—.

Vanity, saith the preacher, vanity!
Draw round my bed: is Anselm keeping back?
Nephews—sons mine . . . ah God, I know not! Well—
She, men would have to be your mother once,
Old Gandolf envied me, so fair she was!
What's done is done, and she is dead beside,
Dead long ago, and I am Bishop since,
And as she died so must we die ourselves,
And thence ye may perceive the world's a dream.
Life, how and what is it? As here I lie   10
In this state-chamber, dying by degrees,
Hours and long hours in the dead night, I ask
'Do I live, am I dead?' Peace, peace seems all.
Saint Praxed's ever was the church for peace;
And so, about this tomb of mine. I fought
With tooth and nail to save my niche, ye know:
—Old Gandolf cozened me, despite my care;
Shrewd was that snatch from out the corner South
He graced his carrion with, God curse the same!
Yet still my niche is not so cramped but thence   20
One sees the pulpit o' the epistle-side,
And somewhat of the choir, those silent seats,
And up into the aery dome where live
The angels, and a sunbeam's sure to lurk:
And I shall fill my slab of basalt there,
And 'neath my tabernacle take my rest,

20

With those nine columns round me, two and two,
The odd one at my feet where Anselm stands:
Peach-blossom marble all, the rare, the ripe
As fresh-poured red wine of a mighty pulse. 30
—Old Gandolf with his paltry onion-stone,
Put me where I may look at him! True peach,
Rosy and flawless: how I earned the prize!
Draw close: that conflagration of my church
—What then? So much was saved if aught were missed!
My sons, ye would not be my death? Go dig
The white-grape vineyard where the oil-press stood,
Drop water gently till the surface sink,
And if ye find . . . Ah God, I know not, I! . . .
Bedded in store of rotten fig-leaves soft, 40
And corded up in a tight olive-frail,
Some lump, ah God, of *lapis lazuli*,
Big as a Jew's head cut off at the nape,
Blue as a vein o'er the Madonna's breast . . .
Sons, all have I bequeathed you, villas, all,
That brave Frascati villa with its bath,
So, let the blue lump poise between my knees,
Like God the Father's globe on both his hands
Ye worship in the Jesu Church so gay,
For Gandolf shall not choose but see and burst! 50
Swift as a weaver's shuttle fleet our years:
Man goeth to the grave, and where is he?
Did I say basalt for my slab, sons? Black—
'Twas ever antique-black I meant! How else
Shall ye contrast my frieze to come beneath?
The bas-relief in bronze ye promised me,
Those Pans and Nymphs ye wot of, and perchance
Some tripod, thyrsus, with a vase or so,
The Saviour at his sermon on the mount,
Saint Praxed in a glory, and one Pan 60
Ready to twitch the Nymph's last garment off,

And Moses with the tables . . . but I know
Ye mark me not! What do they whisper thee,
Child of my bowels, Anselm? Ah, ye hope
To revel down my villas while I gasp
Bricked o'er with beggar's mouldy travertine
Which Gandolf from his tomb-top chuckles at!
Nay, boys, ye love me—all of jasper, then!
'Tis jasper ye stand pledged to, lest I grieve.
My bath must needs be left behind, alas!   70
One block, pure green as a pistachio-nut,
There's plenty jasper somewhere in the world—
And have I not Saint Praxed's ear to pray
Horses for ye, and brown Greek manuscripts,
And mistresses with great smooth marbly limbs?
—That's if ye carve my epitaph aright,
Choice Latin, picked phrase, Tully's every word,
No gaudy ware like Gandolf's second line—
Tully, my masters? Ulpian serves his need!
And then how I shall lie through centuries,   80
And hear the blessed mutter of the mass,
And see God made and eaten all day long,
And feel the steady candle-flame, and taste
Good strong thick stupefying incense-smoke!
For as I lie here, hours of the dead night,
Dying in state and by such slow degrees,
I fold my arms as if they clasped a crook,
And stretch my feet forth straight as stone can point,
And let the bedclothes, for a mortcloth, drop
Into great laps and folds of sculptor's-work: 90
And as yon tapers dwindle, and strange thoughts
Grow, with a certain humming in my ears,
About the life before I lived this life,
And this life too, popes, cardinals and priests,
Saint Praxed at his sermon on the mount,
Your tall pale mother with her talking eyes,

And new-found agate urns as fresh as day,
And marble's language, Latin pure, discreet,
—Aha, ELUCESCEBAT quoth our friend?
No Tully, said I, Ulpian at the best!   100
Evil and brief hath been my pilgrimage.
All *lapis*, all, sons! Else I give the Pope
My villas! Will ye ever eat my heart?
Ever your eyes were as a lizard's quick,
They glitter like your mother's for my soul,
Or ye would heighten my impoverished frieze,
Piece out its starved design, and fill my vase
With grapes, and add a vizor and a Term,
And to the tripod ye would tie a lynx
That in his struggle throws the thyrsus down,   110
To comfort me on my entablature
Whereon I am to lie till I must ask
'Do I live, am I dead?' There, leave me, there!
For ye have stabbed me with ingratitude
To death—ye wish it—God, ye wish it! Stone—
Gritstone, a-crumble! Clammy squares which sweat
As if the corpse they keep were oozing through—
And no more *lapis* to delight the world!
Well go! I bless ye. Fewer tapers there,
But in a row: and, going, turn your backs   120
—Ay, like departing altar-ministrants,
And leave me in my church, the church for peace,
That I may watch at leisure if he leers—
Old Gandolf, at me, from his onion-stone,
As still he envied me, so fair she was!

A Woman's Last Word

1

Let's contend no more, Love,
　Strive nor weep:
All be as before, Love,
　—Only sleep!

2

What so wild as words are?
　I and thou
In debate, as birds are,
　Hawk on bough!

3

See the creature stalking
　While we speak!
Hush and hide the talking,
　Cheek on cheek!

4

What so false as truth is,
　False to thee?
Where the serpent's tooth is
　Shun the tree—

5

Where the apple reddens
　Never pry—
Lest we lose our Edens,
　Eve and I.

6

Be a god and hold me
  With a charm!
Be a man and fold me
  With thine arm!

7

Teach me, only teach, Love! ₂⁷
  As I ought
I will speak thy speech, Love,
  Think thy thought—

8

Meet, if thou require it,
  Both demands,
Laying flesh and spirit
  In thy hands.

9

That shall be to-morrow
  Not to-night:
I must bury sorrow
  Out of sight:

10

—Must a little weep, Love,
  (Foolish me!)
And so fall asleep, Love,
  Loved by thee.

Love Among the Ruins

Where the quiet-coloured end of evening smiles,
                    Miles and miles
On the solitary pastures where our sheep
                    Half-asleep
Tinkle homeward thro' the twilight, stray or stop
                    As they crop—
Was the site once of a city great and gay,
                    (So they say)
Of our country's very capital, its prince
                    Ages since
Held his court in, gathered councils, wielding far
                    Peace or war.

2

Now,—the country does not even boast a tree,
                    As you see,
To distinguish slopes of verdure, certain rills
                    From the hills
Intersect and give a name to, (else they run
                    Into one)
Where the domed and daring palace shot its spires
                    Up like fires
O'er the hundred-gated circuit of a wall
                    Bounding all,
Made of marble, men might march on nor be pressed,
                    Twelve abreast.

And such plenty and perfection, see, of grass
      Never was!
Such a carpet as, this summer-time, o'erspreads
      And embeds
Every vestige of the city, guessed alone,
      Stock or stone—
Where a multitude of men breathed joy and woe
      Long ago;
Lust of glory pricked their hearts up, dread of shame
      Struck them tame;
And that glory and that shame alike, the gold
      Bought and sold.

4

Now,—the single little turret that remains
      On the plains,
By the caper overrooted, by the gourd
      Overscored,
While the patching houseleek's head of blossom winks
      Through the chinks—
Marks the basement whence a tower in ancient time
      Sprang sublime,
And a burning ring, all round, the chariots traced
      As they raced,
And the monarch and his minions and his dames
      Viewed the games.

5

And I know, while thus the quiet-coloured eve
      Smiles to leave
To their folding, all our many-tinkling fleece
      In such peace,
And the slopes and rills in undistinguished grey
      Melt away—

That a girl with eager eyes and yellow hair
                    Waits me there
In the turret whence the charioteers caught soul
                    For the goal,
When the king looked, where she looks now, breathless,
        dumb
                    Till I come.

6

But he looked upon the city, every side,
                    Far and wide,
All the mountains topped with temples, all the glades'
                    Colonnades,
All the causeys, bridges, aqueducts,—and then,
                    All the men!
When I do come, she will speak not, she will stand,
                    Either hand
On my shoulder, give her eyes the first embrace
                    Of my face,
Ere we rush, ere we extinguish sight and speech
                    Each on each.

7

In one year they sent a million fighters forth
                    South and North,
And they built their gods a brazen pillar high
                    As the sky,
Yet reserved a thousand chariots in full force—
                    Gold, of course.
Oh heart! oh blood that freezes, blood that burns!
                    Earth's returns
For whole centuries of folly, noise and sin!
                    Shut them in,
With their triumphs and their glories and the rest
                    Love is best.

A Lovers' Quarrel

1

Oh, what a dawn of day!
How the March sun feels like May!
    All is blue again
    After last night's rain,
And the South dries the hawthorn-spray.
    Only, my Love's away!
I'd as lief that the blue were grey.

2

Runnels, which rillets swell,
Must be dancing down the dell,
    With a foaming head
    On the beryl bed
Paven smooth as a hermit's cell;
    Each with a tale to tell,
Could my Love but attend as well.

3

Dearest, three months ago!
When we lived blocked-up with snow,—
    When the wind would edge
    In and in his wedge,
In, as far as the point could go—
    Not to our ingle, though,
Where we loved each the other so!

4

Laughs with so little cause!
We devised games out of straws.
    We would try and trace
    One another's face
In the ash, as an artist draws;
    Free on each other's flaws,
How we chattered like two church daws!

5

What's in the 'Times'?—a scold
At the Emperor deep and cold;
    He has taken a bride
    To his gruesome side,
That's as fair as himself is bold:
    There they sit ermine-stoled,
And she powders her hair with gold.

6

Fancy the Pampas' sheen!
Miles and miles of gold and green
    Where the sunflowers blow
    In a solid glow,
And—to break now and then the screen—
    Black neck and eyeballs keen,
Up a wild horse leaps between!

7

Try, will our table turn?
Lay your hands there light, and yearn
    Till the yearning slips
    Thro' the finger-tips
In a fire which a few discern,
    And a very few feel burn,
And the rest, they may live and learn!

Then we would up and pace,
For a change, about the place,
　　Each with arm o'er neck:
　　'Tis our quarter-deck,
We are seamen in woeful case.
　　Help in the ocean-space!
Or, if no help, we'll embrace.

See, how she looks now, dressed
In a sledging-cap and vest!
　　'Tis a huge fur cloak—
　　Like a reindeer's yoke
Falls the lappet along the breast:
　　Sleeves for her arms to rest,
Or to hang, as my Love likes best.

Teach me to flirt a fan
As the Spanish ladies can,
　　Or I tint your lip
　　With a burnt stick's tip
And you turn into such a man!
　　Just the two spots that span
Half the bill of the young male swan.

Dearest, three months ago
When the mesmerizer Snow
　　With his hand's first sweep
　　Put the earth to sleep:
'Twas a time when the heart could show
　　All—how was earth to know,
'Neath the mute hand's to-and-fro?

Dearest, three months ago
When we loved each other so,
    Lived and loved the same
    Till an evening came
When a shaft from the devil's bow
    Pierced to our ingle-glow,
And the friends were friend and foe!

Not from the heart beneath—
'Twas a bubble born of breath,
    Neither sneer nor vaunt,
    Nor reproach nor taunt.
See a word, how it severeth!
    Oh, power of life and death
In the tongue, as the Preacher saith!

Woman, and will you cast
For a word, quite off at last
    Me, your own, your You,—
    Since, as truth is true,
I was You all the happy past—
    Me do you leave aghast
With the memories We amassed?

Love, if you knew the light
That your soul casts in my sight,
    How I look to you
    For the pure and true
And the beauteous and the right,—
    Bear with a moment's spite
When a mere mote threats the white

16

What of a hasty word?
Is the fleshly heart not stirred
　　By a worm's pin-prick
　　Where its roots are quick?
See the eye, by a fly's foot blurred—
　　Ear, when a straw is heard
Scratch the brain's coat of curd!

17

Foul be the world or fair
More or less, how can I care?
　　'Tis the world the same
　　For my praise or blame,
And endurance is easy there.
　　Wrong in the one thing rare—
Oh, it is hard to bear!

18

Here's the spring back or close,
When the almond-blossom blows:
　　We shall have the word
　　In a minor third
There is none but the cuckoo knows:
　　Heaps of the guelder-rose!
I must bear with it, I suppose.

19

Could but November come,
Were the noisy birds struck dumb
　　At the warning slash
　　Of his driver's-lash—
I would laugh like the valiant Thumb
　　Facing the castle glum
And the giant's fee-faw-fum!

Then, were the world well stripped
Of the gear wherein equipped
    We can stand apart,
    Heart dispense with heart
In the sun, with the flowers unnipped,—
    Oh, the world's hangings ripped,
We were both in a bare-walled crypt!

21

Each in the crypt would cry
'But one freezes here! and why?
    'When a heart, as chill,
    'At my own would thrill
'Back to life, and its fires out-fly?
    'Heart, shall we live or die?
'The rest, . . . settle by-and-by!'

22

So, she'd efface the score,
And forgive me as before.
    It is twelve o'clock:
    I shall hear her knock
In the worst of a storm's uproar,
    I shall pull her through the door,
I shall have her for evermore!

Up at a Villa—Down in the City

(As distinguished by an Italian person of quality)

I

Had I but plenty of money, money enough and to spare,
The house for me, no doubt, were a house in the city-square;
Ah, such a life, such a life, as one leads at the window there!

Something to see, by Bacchus, something to hear, at least!
There, the whole day long, one's life is a perfect feast;
While up at a villa one lives, I maintain it, no more than a
beast.

Well now, look at our villa! stuck like the horn of a bull
Just on a mountain-edge as bare as the creature's skull,
Save a mere shag of a bush with hardly a leaf to pull!
—I scratch my own, sometimes, to see if the hair's turned wool.

But the city, oh the city—the square with the houses! Why?
They are stone-faced, white as a curd, there's something to take
the eye!
Houses in four straight lines, not a single front awry;
You watch who crosses and gossips, who saunters, who hurries
by;
Green blinds, as a matter of course, to draw when the sun gets
high;
And the shops with fanciful signs which are painted properly.

What of a villa? Though winter be over in March by rights,
'Tis May perhaps ere the snow shall have withered well off the
heights:
You've the brown ploughed land before, where the oxen steam
and wheeze,
And the hills over-smoked behind by the faint grey olive-trees.

Is it better in May, I ask you? You've summer all at once;
In a day he leaps complete with a few strong April suns.
'Mid the sharp short emerald wheat, scarce risen three fingers
well,

The wild tulip, at end of its tube, blows out its great red bell
Like a thin clear bubble of blood, for the children to pick and
    sell.

7

Is it ever hot in the square? There's a fountain to spout and
    splash!
In the shade it sings and springs; in the shine such foam-bows
    flash
On the horses with curling fish-tails, that prance and paddle and
    pash
Round the lady atop in her conch—fifty gazers do not abash,
Though all that she wears is some weeds round her waist in a
    sort of sash.

8

All the year long at the villa, nothing to see though you linger,
Except yon cypress that points like death's lean lifted forefinger.
Some think fireflies pretty, when they mix i' the corn and
    mingle,
Or thrid the stinking hemp till the stalks of it seem a-tingle.
Late August or early September, the stunning cicala is shrill,
And the bees keep their tiresome whine round the resinous firs
    on the hill.
Enough of the seasons,—I spare you the months of the fever
    and chill.

9

Ere you open your eyes in the city, the blessed church-bells
    begin:
No sooner the bells leave off than the diligence rattles in:
You get the pick of the news, and it costs you never a pin.
By-and-by there's the travelling doctor gives pills, lets blood,
    draws teeth;

Or the Pulcinello-trumpet breaks up the market beneath.

At the post-office such a scene-picture—the new play, piping
hot!

And a notice how, only this morning, three liberal thieves were
shot.

Above it, behold the Archbishop's most fatherly of rebukes,

And beneath, with his crown and his lion, some little new law
of the Duke's!

Or a sonnet with flowery marge, to the Reverend Don So-
and-so

Who is Dante, Boccaccio, Petrarca, Saint Jerome and Cicero,

'And moreover,' (the sonnet goes rhyming,) 'the skirts of Saint
Paul has reached,

'Having preached us those six Lent-lectures more unctuous than
ever he preached.'

Noon strikes,—here sweeps the procession! our Lady borne
smiling and smart

With a pink gauze gown all spangles, and seven swords stuck
in her heart!

Bang-whang-whang goes the drum, *tootle-te-tootle* the fife;

No keeping one's haunches still: it's the greatest pleasure in life.

10

But bless you, it's dear—it's dear! fowls, wine, at double the
rate.

They have clapped a new tax upon salt, and what oil pays
passing the gate

It's a horror to think of. And so, the villa for me, not the city!

Beggars can scarcely be choosers: but still—ah, the pity, the
pity!

Look, two and two go the priests, then the monks with cowls
and sandals,

And the penitents dressed in white shirts, a-holding the yellow
candles;

37

One, he carries a flag up straight, and another a cross with
    handles,
And the Duke's guard brings up the rear, for the better pre-
    vention of scandals:
Bang-whang-whang goes the drum, tootle-te-tootle the fife.
Oh, a day in the city-square, there is no such pleasure in life!

A Toccata of Galuppi's

1

Oh Galuppi, Baldassaro, this is very sad to find!
I can hardly misconceive you; it would prove me deaf and
    blind;
But although I take your meaning, 'tis with such a heavy mind!

2

Here you come with your old music, and here's all the good it
    brings.
What, they lived once thus at Venice where the merchants were
    the kings,
Where Saint Mark's is, where the Doges used to wed the sea
    with rings?

3

Ay, because the sea's the street there; and 'tis arched by . . .
    what you call
. . . Shylock's bridge with houses on it, where they kept the
    carnival:
I was never out of England—it's as if I saw it all.

4

Did young people take their pleasure when the sea was warm
in May?

Balls and masks begun at midnight, burning ever to mid-day,

When they made up fresh adventures for the morrow, do you
say?

5

Was a lady such a lady, cheeks so round and lips so red,—

On her neck the small face buoyant, like a bell-flower on its
bed,

O'er the breast's superb abundance where a man might base his
head?

6

Well, and it was graceful of them—they'd break talk off and
afford

—She, to bite her mask's black velvet—he, to finger on his
sword,

While you sat and played Toccatas, stately at the clavichord?

7

What? Those lesser thirds so plaintive, sixths diminished, sigh
on sigh,

Told them something? Those suspensions, those solutions—
'Must we die?'

Those commiserating sevenths—'Life might last! we can but
try!'

8

'Were you happy?'—'Yes.'—'And are you still as happy?'—
'Yes. And you?'

—'Then, more kisses!'—'Did *I* stop them, when a million
seemed so few?'

Hark, the dominant's persistence till it must be answered to!

So, an octave struck the answer. Oh, they praised you, I dare
    say!
'Brave Galuppi! that was music! good alike at grave and gay!
'I can always leave off talking when I hear a master play!'

Then they left you for their pleasure: till in due time, one by
    one,
Some with lives that came to nothing, some with deeds as well
    undone,
Death stepped tacitly and took them where they never see the
    sun.

But when I sit down to reason, think to take my stand nor
    swerve,
While I triumph o'er a secret wrung from nature's close reserve,
In you come with your cold music till I creep thro' every nerve.

Yes, you, like a ghostly cricket, creaking where a house was
    burned:
'Dust and ashes, dead and done with, Venice spent what Venice
    earned.
'The soul, doubtless, is immortal—where a soul can be dis-
    cerned.

'Yours for instance: you know physics, something of geology,
'Mathematics are your pastime; souls shall rise in their degree;
'Butterflies may dread extinction,—you'll not die, it cannot be!

'As for Venice and her people, merely born to bloom and drop,
'Here on earth they bore their fruitage, mirth and folly were the
    crop:
'What of soul was left, I wonder, when the kissing had to stop?

'Dust and ashes!' So you creak it, and I want the heart to scold.
Dear dead women, with such hair, too—what's become of all
    the gold
Used to hang and brush their bosoms? I feel chilly and grown
    old.

'De Gustibus——'

Your ghost will walk, you lover of trees,
        (If our loves remain)
        In an English lane,
By a cornfield-side a-flutter with poppies.
Hark, those two in the hazel coppice—
A boy and a girl, if the good fates please,
        Making love, say,—
        The happier they!
Draw yourself up from the light of the moon,
And let them pass, as they will too soon,
        With the bean-flowers' boon,
        And the blackbird's tune,
        And May, and June!

What I love best in all the world
Is a castle, precipice-encurled,
In a gash of the wind-grieved Apennine
Or look for me, old fellow of mine.

(If I get my head from out the mouth
O' the grave, and loose my spirit's bands,
And come again to the land of lands)—
In a sea-side house to the farther South,
Where the baked cicala dies of drouth,
And one sharp tree—'tis a cypress—stands,
By the many hundred years red-rusted,
Rough iron-spiked, ripe fruit-o'ercrusted,
My sentinel to guard the sands
To the water's edge. For, what expands
Before the house, but the great opaque
Blue breadth of sea without a break?
While, in the house, for ever crumbles
Some fragment of the frescoed walls,
From blisters where a scorpion sprawls.
A girl bare-footed brings, and tumbles
Down on the pavement, green-flesh melons,
And says there's news to-day—the king
Was shot at, touched in the liver-wing,
Goes with his Bourbon arm in a sling:
—She hopes they have not caught the felons.
Italy, my Italy!
Queen Mary's saying serves for me—
　　　(When fortune's malice
　　　Lost her—Calais)—
Open my heart and you will see
Graved inside of it, 'Italy.'
Such lovers old are I and she:
So it always was, so shall ever be!

By the Fireside

1

How well I know what I mean to do
  When the long dark autumn-evenings come:
And where, my soul, is thy pleasant hue?
  With the music of all thy voices, dumb
In life's November too!

2

I shall be found by the fire, suppose,
  O'er a great wise book as beseemeth age,
While the shutters flap as the cross-wind blows
  And I turn the page, and I turn the page,
Not verse now, only prose!

3

Till the young ones whisper, finger on lip,
  'There he is at it, deep in Greek:
'Now then, or never, out we slip
  'To cut from the hazels by the creek
'A mainmast for our ship!'

4

I shall be at it indeed, my friends:
  Greek puts already on either side
Such a branch-work forth as soon extends
  To a vista opening far and wide,
And I pass out where it ends.

5

The outside-frame, like your hazel-trees;
　But the inside-archway widens fast,
And a rarer sort succeeds to these,
　And we slope to Italy at last
And youth, by green degrees.

6

I follow wherever I am led,
　Knowing so well the leader's hand:
Oh woman-country, wooed not wed,
　Loved all the more by earth's male-lands,
Laid to their hearts instead!

7

Look at the ruined chapel again
　Half-way up in the Alpine gorge!
Is that a tower, I point you plain,
　Or is it a mill, or an iron-forge
Breaks solitude in vain?

8

A turn, and we stand in the heart of things;
　The woods are round us, heaped and dim;
From slab to slab how it slips and springs,
　The thread of water single and slim,
Through the ravage some torrent brings!

9

Does it feed the little lake below?
　That speck of white just on its marge
Is Pella; see, in the evening-glow,
　How sharp the silver spear-heads charge
When Alp meets heaven in snow!

On our other side is the straight-up rock;
　And a path is kept 'twixt the gorge and it
By boulder-stones where lichens mock
　The marks on a moth, and small ferns fit
Their teeth to the polished block.

Oh the sense of the yellow mountain-flowers,
　And thorny balls, each three in one,
The chestnuts throw on our path in showers!
　For the drop of the woodland fruit's begun,
These early November hours,

That crimson the creeper's leaf across
　Like a splash of blood, intense, abrupt,
O'er a shield else gold from rim to boss,
　And lay it for show on the fairy-cupped
Elf-needled mat of moss,

By the rose-flesh mushrooms, undivulged
　Last evening　nay, in to-day's first dew
Yon sudden coral nipple bulged,
　Where a freaked fawn-coloured flaky crew
Of toadstools peep indulged.

And yonder, at foot of the fronting ridge
　That takes the turn to a range beyond,
Is the chapel reached by the one-arched bridge
　Where the water is stopped in a stagnant pond
Danced over by the midge.

15

The chapel and bridge are of stone alike,
    Blackish-grey and mostly wet;
Cut hemp-stalks steep in the narrow dyke.
    See here again, how the lichens fret
And the roots of the ivy strike!

16

Poor little place, where its one priest comes
    On a festa-day, if he comes at all,
To the dozen folk from their scattered homes,
    Gathered within that precinct small
By the dozen ways one roams—

17

To drop from the charcoal-burners' huts,
    Or climb from the hemp-dressers' low shed,
Leave the grange where the woodman stores his nuts,
    Or the wattled cote where the fowlers spread
Their gear on the rock's bare juts.

18

It has some pretension too, this front,
    With its bit of fresco half-moon-wise
Set over the porch, Art's early wont:
    'Tis John in the Desert, I surmise,
But has borne the weather's brunt—

19

Not from the fault of the builder, though,
    For a pent-house properly projects
Where three carved beams make a certain show,
    Dating—good thought of our architect's—
'Five, six, nine, he lets you know.

And all day long a bird sings there,
  And a stray sheep drinks at the pond at times;
The place is silent and aware;
  It has had its scenes, its joys and crimes,
But that is its own affair.

My perfect wife, my Leonor,
  Oh heart, my own, oh eyes, mine too,
Whom else could I dare look backward for,
  With whom beside should I dare pursue
The path grey heads abhor?

For it leads to a crag's sheer edge with them;
  Youth, flowery all the way, there stops—
Not they; age threatens and they contemn,
  Till they reach the gulf wherein youth drops,
One inch from life's safe hem!

With me, youth led . . . I will speak now,
  No longer watch you as you sit
Reading by fire-light, that great brow
  And the spirit-small hand propping it,
Mutely, my heart knows how—

When, if I think but deep enough,
  You are wont to answer, prompt as rhyme;
And you, too, find without rebuff
  Response your soul seeks many a time
Piercing its fine flesh-stuff.

My own, confirm me! If I tread
   This path back, is it not in pride
To think how little I dreamed it led
   Tu ... ..., ...,
Youth seems the waste instead?

26

My own, see where the years conduct!
   At first, 'twas something our two souls
Should mix as mists do; each is sucked
   In each now: on, the new stream rolls,
Whatever rocks obstruct.

27

Think, when our one soul understands
   The great Word which makes all things new,
When earth breaks up and heaven expands,
   How will the change strike me and you
In the house not made with hands?

28

Oh I must feel your brain prompt mine,
   Your heart anticipate my heart,
You must be just before, in fine,
   See and make me see, for your part,
New depths of the divine!

29

But who could have expected this
   When we two drew together first
Just for the obvious human bliss,
   To satisfy life's daily thirst
With a thing men seldom miss?

Come back with me to the first of all,
　　Let us lean and love it over again,
Let us now forget and now recall,
　　Break the rosary in a pearly rain,
And gather what we let fall!

What did I say?—that a small bird sings
　　All day long, save when a brown pair
Of hawks from the wood float with wide wings
　　Strained to a bell: 'gainst noon-day glare
You count the streaks and rings.

But at afternoon or almost eve
　　'Tis better; then the silence grows
To that degree, you half believe
　　It must get rid of what it knows,
Its bosom does so heave.

Hither we walked then, side by side,
　　Arm in arm and cheek to cheek,
And still I questioned or replied,
　　While my heart, convulsed to really speak,
Lay choking in its pride.

Silent the crumbling bridge we cross,
　　And pity and praise the chapel sweet,
And care about the fresco's loss,
　　And wish for our souls a like retreat,
And wonder at the moss.

35

Stoop and kneel on the settle under,
    Look through the window's grated square:
Nothing to see! For fear of plunder,
    The cross is down and the altar bare,
As if thieves don't fear thunder.

36

We stoop and look in through the grate,
    See the little porch and rustic door,
Read duly the dead builder's date;
    Then cross the bridge that we crossed before,
Take the path again—but wait!

37

Oh moment, one and infinite!
    The water slips o'er stock and stone;
The West is tender, hardly bright:
    How grey at once is the evening grown—
One star, its chrysolite!

38

We two stood there with never a third,
    But each by each, as each knew well:
The sights we saw and the sounds we heard,
    The lights and the shades made up a spell
Till the trouble grew and stirred.

39

Oh, the little more, and how much it is!
    And the little less, and what worlds away!
How a sound shall quicken content to bliss,
    Or a breath suspend the blood's best play,
And life be a proof of this!

Had she willed it, still had stood the screen
 So slight, so sure, 'twixt my love and her:
I could fix her face with a guard between,
 And find her soul as when friends confer,
Friends—lovers that might have been.

For my heart had a touch of the woodland-time,
 Wanting to sleep now over its best.
Shake the whole tree in the summer-prime,
 But bring to the last leaf no such test!
'Hold the last fast!' runs the rhyme.

For a chance to make your little much,
 To gain a lover and lose a friend,
Venture the tree and a myriad such,
 When nothing you mar but the year can mend:
But a last leaf—fear to touch!

Yet should it unfasten itself and fall
 Eddying down till it find your face
At some slight wind—best chance of all!
 Be your heart henceforth its dwelling-place
You trembled to forestall!

Worth how well, those dark grey eyes,
 That hair so dark and dear, how worth
That a man should strive and agonise,
 And taste a veriest hell on earth
For the hope of such a prize!

45

You might have turned and tried a man,
  Set him a space to weary and wear,
And prove which suited more your plan,
  His best of hope or his worst despair,
Yet end as he began.

46

But you spared me this, like the heart you are,
  And filled my empty heart at a word.
If two lives join, there is oft a scar,
  They are one and one, with a shadowy third;
One near one is too far.

47

A moment after, and hands unseen
  Were hanging the night around us fast;
But we knew that a bar was broken between
  Life and life: we were mixed at last
In spite of the mortal screen.

48

The forests had done it; there they stood;
  We caught for a moment the powers at play:
They had mingled us so, for once and good,
  Their work was done—we might go or stay,
They relapsed to their ancient mood.

49

How the world is made for each of us!
  How all we perceive and know in it
Tends to some moment's product thus,
  When a soul declares itself—to wit,
By its fruit, the thing it does!

52

Be hate that fruit or love that fruit,
    It forwards the general deed of man,
And each of the Many helps to recruit
The life of the race by a general plan;
Each living his own, to boot.

I am named and known by that moment's feat;
    There took my station and degree;
So grew my own small life complete,
    As nature obtained her best of me—
One born to love you, sweet.

And to watch you sink by the fire-side now
    Back again, as you mutely sit
Musing by fire light, that great brow
    And the spirit-small hand propping it,
Yonder, my heart knows how!

So, earth has gained by one man the more,
    And the gain of earth must be heaven's gain too;
And the whole is well worth thinking o'er
When autumn comes: which I mean to do
    One day, as I said before.

Two in the Campagna

I

I wonder do you feel to-day
   As I have felt since, hand in hand,
We sat down on the grass, to stray
   In spirit better through the land,
This morn of Rome and May?

2

For me, I touched a thought, I know,
   Has tantalised me many times,
(Like turns of thread the spiders throw
   Mocking across our path) for rhymes
To catch at and let go.

3

Help me to hold it! First it left
   The yellowing fennel, run to seed
There, branching from the brickwork's cleft,
   Some old tomb's ruin: yonder weed
Took up the floating weft,

4

Where one small orange cup amassed
   Five beetles,—blind and green they grope
Among the honey-meal: and last,
   Everywhere on the grassy slope
I traced it. Hold it fast!

5

The champaign with its endless fleece
　　Of feathery grasses everywhere!
Silence and passion, joy and peace,
　　An everlasting wash of air—
Rome's ghost since her decease.

6

Such life here, through such lengths of hours,
　　Such miracles performed in play,
Such primal naked forms of flowers,
　　Such letting nature have her way
While heaven looks from its towers!

7

How say you? Let us, O my dove,
　　Let us be unashamed of soul,
As earth lies bare to heaven above!
　　How is it under our control
To love or not to love?

8

I would that you were all to me,
　　You that are just so much, no more.
Nor yours nor mine, nor slave nor free!
　　Where does the fault lie? What the core
O' the wound, since wound must be?

9

I would I could adopt your will,
　　See with your eyes, and set my heart
Beating by yours, and drink my fill
　　At your soul's springs,—your part my part
In life, for good and ill.

No. I yearn upward, touch you close,
   Then stand away. I kiss your cheek,
Catch your soul's warmth,—I pluck the rose
   And love it more than tongue can speak—
Then the good minute goes.

Already how am I so far
   Out of that minute? Must I go
Still like the thistle-ball, no bar,
   Onward, whenever light winds blow,
Fixed by no friendly star?

Just when I seemed about to learn!
   Where is the thread now? Off again!
The old trick! Only I discern—
   Infinite passion, and the pain
Of finite hearts that yearn.

Misconceptions

This is a spray the Bird clung to,
   Making it blossom with pleasure,
Ere the high tree-top she sprung to,
   Fit for her nest and her treasure.
   Oh, what a hope beyond measure
Was the poor spray's, which the flying feet hung to,—
So to be singled out, built in, and sung to!

This is a heart the Queen leant on,
　　Thrilled in a minute erratic,
Ere the true bosom she bent on,
　　Meet for love's regal dalmatic.
　　Oh, what a fancy ecstatic
Was the poor heart's, ere the wanderer went on—
Love to be saved for it, proffered to, spent on!

Memorabilia

Ah, did you once see Shelley plain,
　　And did he stop and speak to you
And did you speak to him again?
　　How strange it seems and new!

But you were living before that,
　　And also you are living after;
And the memory I started at—
　　My starting moves your laughter.

I crossed a moor, with a name of its own
　　And a certain use in the world no doubt,
Yet a hand's-breadth of it shines alone
　　'Mid the blank miles round about:

For there I picked up on the heather
　　And there I put inside my breast
A moulted feather, an eagle-feather!
　　Well, I forget the rest.

Popularity

1

Stand still, true poet that you are!
  I know you; let me try and draw you.
Some night you'll fail us: when afar
  You rise, remember one man saw you,
Knew you, and named a star!

2

My star, God's glow-worm! Why extend
  That loving hand of his which leads you
Yet locks you safe from end to end
  Of this dark world, unless he needs you,
Just saves your light to spend?

3

His clenched hand shall unclose at last,
  I know, and let out all the beauty:
My poet holds the future fast,
  Accepts the coming ages' duty,
Their present for this past.

4

That day, the earth's feast-master's brow
  Shall clear, to God the chalice raising;
'Others give best at first, but thou
  'Forever set'st our table praising,
'Keep'st the good wine till now!'

5

Meantime, I'll draw you as you stand,
  With few or none to watch and wonder:
I'll say—a fisher, on the sand
  By Tyre the old, with ocean-plunder,
A netful, brought to land.

6

Who has not heard how Tyrian shells
  Enclosed the blue, that dye of dyes
Whereof one drop worked miracles,
  And coloured like Astarte's eyes
Raw silk the merchant sells?

7

And each bystander of them all
  Could criticise, and quote tradition
How depths of blue sublimed some pall
  —To get which, pricked a king's ambition;
Worth sceptre, crown and ball.

8

Yet there's the dye, in that rough mesh,
  The sea has only just o'erwhispered!
Live whelks, each lip's beard dripping fresh,
  As if they still the water's lisp heard
Through foam the rock-weeds thresh.

9

Enough to furnish Solomon
  Such hangings for his cedar-house,
That, when gold-robed he took the throne
  In that abyss of blue, the Spouse
Might swear his presence shone

Most like the centre-spike of gold
  Which burns deep in the blue-bell's womb,
What time, with ardours manifold,
  The bee goes singing to her groom,
Drunken and overbold.

Mere conchs! not fit for warp or woof!
  Till cunning come to pound and squeeze
And clarify,—refine to proof
  The liquor filtered by degrees,
While the world stands aloof.

And there's the extract, flasked and fine,
  And priced and saleable at last!
And Hobbs, Nobbs, Stokes and Nokes combine
  To paint the future from the past,
Put blue into their line.

Hobbs hints blue,—straight he turtle eats:
  Nobbs prints blue,—claret crowns his cup:
Nokes outdares Stokes in azure feats,—
  Both gorge. Who fished the murex up?
What porridge had John Keats?

A Light Woman

1

So far as our story approaches the end,
    Which do you pity the most of us three?—
My friend, or the mistress of my friend
    With her wanton eyes, or me?

2

My friend was already too good to lose,
    And seemed in the way of improvement yet,
When she crossed his path with her hunting-noose
    And over him drew her net.

3

When I saw him tangled in her toils,
    A shame, said I, if she adds just him
To her nine-and-ninety other spoils,
    The hundredth for a whim!

4

And before my friend be wholly hers,
    How easy to prove to him, I said,
An eagle's the game her pride prefers,
    Though she snaps at a wren instead!

5

So, I gave her eyes my own eyes to take,
    My hand sought hers as in earnest need,
And round she turned for my noble sake
    And gave me herself indeed.

6

The eagle am I, with my fame in the world,
   The wren is he, with his maiden face.
—You look away and your lip is curled?
   Patience, a moment's space!

7

For see, my friend goes shaking and white;
   He eyes me as the basilisk:
I have turned, it appears, his day to night,
   Eclipsing his sun's disk.

8

And I did it, he thinks, as a very thief:
   'Though I love her—that, he comprehends—
'One should master one's passions, (love, in chief)
   'And be loyal to one's friends!'

9

And she,—she lies in my hand as tame
   As a pear late basking over a wall;
Just a touch to try and off it came;
   'Tis mine,—can I let it fall?

10

With no mind to eat it, that's the worst!
   Were it thrown in the road, would the case assist?
'Twas quenching a dozen blue-flies' thirst
   When I gave its stalk a twist.

11

And I,—what I seem to my friend, you see:
   What I soon shall seem to his love, you guess:
What I seem to myself, do you ask of me?
   No hero, I confess.

'Tis an awkward thing to play with souls,
  And matter enough to save one's own:
Yet think of my friend, and the burning coals
  He played with for bits of stone!

One likes to show the truth for the truth;
  That the woman was light is very true:
But suppose she says,—Never mind that youth!
  What wrong have I done to you?

Well, any how, here the story stays,
  So far at least as I understand;
And, Robert Browning, you writer of plays,
  Here's a subject made to your hand!

The Last Ride Together

I

I said—Then, dearest, since 'tis so,
Since now at length my fate I know,
Since nothing all my love avails,
Since all, my life seemed meant for, fails,
  Since this was written and needs must be—
My whole heart rises up to bless
Your name in pride and thankfulness!
Take back the hope you gave,—I claim
Only a memory of the same,
—And this beside, if you will not blame,
  Your leave for one more last ride with me.

My mistress bent that brow of hers;
Those deep dark eyes where pride demurs
When pity would be softening through,
Fixed me a breathing-while or two

  With life or death in the balance: right!
The blood replenished me again;
My last thought was at least not vain:
I and my mistress, side by side
Shall be together, breathe and ride,
So, one day more am I deified.
  Who knows but the world may end to-night?

3

Hush! if you saw some western cloud
All billowy-bosomed, over-bowed
By many benedictions—sun's
And moon's and evening-star's at once—

  And so, you, looking and loving best,
Conscious grew, your passion drew
Cloud, sunset, moonrise, star-shine too,
Down on you, near and yet more near,
Till flesh must fade for heaven was here!—
Thus leant she and lingered—joy and fear!
  Thus lay she a moment on my breast.

4

Then we began to ride. My soul
Smoothed itself out, a long-cramped scroll
Freshening and fluttering in the wind.
Past hopes already lay behind.

  What need to strive with a life awry?
Had I said that, had I done this,
So might I gain, so might I miss.

Might she have loved me? just as well
She might have hated, who can tell!
Where had I been now if the worst befell?
    And here we are riding, she and I.

5

Fail I alone, in words and deeds?
Why, all men strive and who succeeds?
We rode; it seemed my spirit flew,
Saw other regions, cities new,
    As the world rushed by on either side.
I thought,—All labour, yet no less
Bear up beneath their unsuccess.
Look at the end of work, contrast
The petty done, the undone vast,
This present of theirs with the hopeful past!
    I hoped she would love me; here we ride.

6

What hand and brain went ever paired?
What heart alike conceived and dared?
What act proved all its thought had been?
What will but felt the fleshly screen?
    We ride and I see her bosom heave.
There's many a crown for who can reach.
Ten lines, a statesman's life in each!
The flag stuck on a heap of bones,
A soldier's doing! what atones?
They scratch his name on the Abbey-stones.
    My riding is better, by their leave.

7

What does it all mean, poet? Well,
Your brains beat into rhythm, you tell

What we felt only; you expressed
You hold things beautiful the best,
    And pace them in rhyme so, side by side.
'Tis something, nay 'tis much: but then,
Have you yourself what's best for men?
Are you—poor, sick, old ere your time—
Nearer one whit your own sublime
Than we who never have turned a rhyme?
    Sing, riding's a joy! For me, I ride.

8

And you, great sculptor—so, you gave
A score of years to Art, her slave,
And that's your Venus, whence we turn
To yonder girl that fords the burn!
    You acquiesce, and shall I repine?
What, man of music, you grown grey
With notes and nothing else to say,
Is this your sole praise from a friend,
'Greatly his opera's strains intend,
'But in music we know how fashions end!'
    I gave my youth; but we ride, in fine.

9

Who knows what's fit for us? Had fate
Proposed bliss here should sublimate
My being—had I signed the bond—
Still one must lead some life beyond,
    Have a bliss to die with, dim-descried.
This foot once planted on the goal,
This glory-garland round my soul,
Could I descry such? Try and test!
I sink back shuddering from the quest.
Earth being so good, would heaven seem best?
    Now, heaven and she are beyond this ride.

10

And yet—she has not spoke so long!
What if heaven be that, fair and strong
At life's best, with our eyes upturned
Whither life's flower is first discerned,
  We, fixed so, ever should so abide?
What if we still ride on, we two
With life for ever old yet new,
Changed not in kind but in degree,
The instant made eternity,—
And heaven just prove that I and she
  Ride, ride together, for ever ride?

'Childe Roland to the Dark Tower Came'

(See Edgar's song in 'LEAR'*)*

1

My first thought was, he lied in every word,
  That hoary cripple, with malicious eye
  Askance to watch the working of his lie
On mine, and mouth scarce able to afford
Suppression of the glee, that pursed and scored
  Its edge, at one more victim gained thereby.

2

What else should he be set for, with his staff?
  What, save to waylay with his lies, ensnare
  All travellers who might find him posted there,
And ask the road? I guessed what skull-like laugh
Would break, what crutch 'gin write my epitaph
  For pastime in the dusty thoroughfare.

3

If at his counsel I should turn aside
  Into that ominous tract which, all agree,
  Hides the Dark Tower. Yet acquiescingly
I did turn as he pointed: neither pride
Nor hope rekindling at the end descried,
  So much as gladness that some end might be.

4

For, what with my whole world-wide wandering,
  What with my search drawn out thro' years, my hope
  Dwindled into a ghost not fit to cope
With that obstreperous joy success would bring,
I hardly tried now to rebuke the spring
  My heart made, finding failure in its scope.

5

As when a sick man very near to death
  Seems dead indeed, and feels begin and end
  The tears and takes the farewell of each friend.
And hears one bid the other go, draw breath
Freelier outside, ('since all is o'er,' he saith,
  'And the blow fallen no grieving can amend;')

6

While some discuss if near the other graves
  Be room enough for this, and when a day
  Suits best for carrying the corpse away,
With care about the banners, scarves and staves:
And still the man hears all, and only craves
  He may not shame such tender love and stay.

Thus, I had so long suffered in this quest,
  Heard failure prophesied so oft, been writ
  So many times among 'The Band'—to wit,
The knights who to the Dark Tower's search addressed
Their steps—that just to fail as they, seemed best,
  And all the doubt was now—should I be fit?

So, quiet as despair, I turned from him,
  That hateful cripple, out of his highway
  Into the path he pointed. All the day
Had been a dreary one at best, and dim
Was settling to its close, yet shot one grim
  Red leer to see the plain catch its estray.

For mark! no sooner was I fairly found
  Pledged to the plain, after a pace or two,
  Than, pausing to throw backward a last view
O'er the safe road, 'twas gone; grey plain all round:
Nothing but plain to the horizon's bound.
  I might go on; nought else remained to do.

So, on I went. I think I never saw
  Such starved ignoble nature; nothing throve:
  For flowers—as well expect a cedar grove!
But cockle, spurge, according to their law
Might propagate their kind, with none to awe,
  You'd think; a burr had been a treasure-trove.

No! penury, inertness and grimace,
  In some strange sort, were the land's portion. 'See
  'Or shut your eyes,' said Nature peevishly,
'It nothing skills: I cannot help my case:
''Tis the Last Judgment's fire must cure this place,
  'Calcine its clods and set my prisoners free.'

If there pushed any ragged thistle-stalk
  Above its mates, the head was chopped; the bents
  Were jealous else. What made those holes and rents
In the dock's harsh swarth leaves, bruised as to baulk
All hope of greenness? 'tis a brute must walk
  Pashing their life out, with a brute's intents.

As for the grass, it grew as scant as hair
  In leprosy; thin dry blades pricked the mud
  Which underneath looked kneaded up with blood.
One stiff blind horse, his every bone a-stare,
Stood stupefied, however he came there:
  Thrust out past service from the devil's stud!

Alive? he might be dead for aught I know,
  With that red gaunt and colloped neck a-strain,
  And shut eyes underneath the rusty mane;
Seldom went such grotesqueness with such woe;
I never saw a brute I hated so;
  He must be wicked to deserve such pain.

I shut my eyes and turned them on my heart.
  As a man calls for wine before he fights,
  I asked one draught of earlier, happier sights,
Ere fitly I could hope to play my part.
Think first, fight afterwards—the soldier's art:
  One taste of the old time sets all to rights.

Not it! I fancied Cuthbert's reddening face
  Beneath its garniture of curly gold,
  Dear fellow, till I almost felt him fold
An arm in mine to fix me to the place,
That way he used. Alas, one night's disgrace!
  Out went my heart's new fire and left it cold.

Giles then, the soul of honour—there he stands
  Frank as ten years ago when knighted first.
  What honest man should dare (he said) he durst.
Good—but the scene shifts—faugh! what hangman hands
Pin to his breasts a parchment? His own bands
  Read it. Poor traitor, spit upon and curst!

Better this present than a past like that;
  Back therefore to my darkening path again!
  No sound, no sight as far as eye could strain.
Will the night send a howlet or a bat?
I asked: when something on the dismal flat
  Came to arrest my thoughts and change their train.

A sudden little river crossed my path
  As unexpected as a serpent comes.
  No sluggish tide congenial to the glooms;
This, as it frothed by, might have been a bath
For the fiend's glowing hoof—to see the wrath
  Of its black eddy bespate with flakes and spumes.

So petty yet so spiteful! All along,
  Low scrubby alders kneeled down over it;
  Drenched willows flung them headlong in a fit
Of mute despair, a suicidal throng:
The river which had done them all the wrong,
  Whate'er that was, rolled by, deterred no whit.

Which, while I forded,—good saints, how I feared
  To set my foot upon a dead man's cheek,
  Each step, or feel the spear I thrust to seek
For hollows, tangled in his hair or beard!
—It may have been a water-rat I speared,
  But, ugh! it sounded like a baby's shriek.

Glad was I when I reached the other bank.
  Nor for a better country. Vain presage!
  Who were the strugglers, what war did they wage,
Whose savage trample thus could pad the dank
Soil to a plash? Toads in a poisoned tank,
  Or wild cats in a red-hot iron cage—

The fight must so have seemed in that fell cirque.
  What penned them there, with all the plain to choose?
  No foot-print leading to that horrid mews,
None out of it. Mad brewage set to work
Their brains, no doubt, like galley-slaves the Turk
  Pits for his pastime, Christians against Jews.

And more than that—a furlong on—why, there!
  What bad use was that engine for, that wheel,
  Or brake, not wheel—that harrow fit to reel
Men's bodies out like silk? with all the air
Of Tophet's tool, on earth left unaware,
  Or brought to sharpen its rusty teeth of steel.

Then came a bit of stubbed ground, once a wood,
  Next a marsh, it would seem, and now mere earth
  Desperate and done with; (so a fool finds mirth,
Makes a thing and then mars it, till his mood
Changes and off he goes!) within a rood—
  Bog, clay and rubble, sand and stark black dearth.

Now blotches rankling, coloured gay and grim,
  Now patches where some leanness of the soil's
  Broke into moss or substances like boils;
Then came some palsied oak, a cleft in him
Like a distorted mouth that splits its rim
  Gaping at death, and dies while it recoils.

And just as far as ever from the end!
  Nought in the distance but the evening, nought
  To point my footstep further! At the thought,
A great black bird, Apollyon's bosom friend,
Sailed past, nor beat his wide wing dragon-penned
  That brushed my cap—perchance the guide I sought.

For, looking up, aware I somehow grew,
  'Spite of the dusk, the plain had given place
  All round to mountains—with such name to grace
Mere ugly heights and heaps now stolen in view.
How thus they had surprised me,—solve it, you!
  How to get from them was no clearer case.

Yet half I seemed to recognise some trick
  Of mischief happened to me, God knows when—
  In a bad dream perhaps. Here ended, then,
Progress this way. When, in the very nick
Of giving up, one time more, came a click
  As when a trap shuts—you're inside the den!

Burningly it came on me all at once,
  This was the place! those two hills on the right,
  Crouched like two bulls locked horn in horn in fight;
While to the left, a tall scalped mountain . . . Dunce,
Dotard, a-dozing at the very nonce,
  After a life spent training for the sight!

31

What in the midst lay but the Tower itself?
  The round squat turret, blind as the fool's heart,
  Built of brown stone, without a counterpart
In the whole world. The tempest's mocking elf
Points to the shipman thus the unseen shelf
  He strikes on, only when the timbers start.

32

Not see? because of night perhaps?—why, day
  Came back again for that! before it left,
  The dying sunset kindled through a cleft:
The hills, like giants at a hunting, lay,
Chin upon hand, to see the game at bay,—
  'Now stab and end the creature—to the heft!'

33

Not hear? when noise was everywhere! it tolled
  Increasing like a bell. Names in my ears
  Of all the lost adventurers my peers,—
How such a one was strong, and such was bold,
And such was fortunate, yet each of old
  Lost, lost! one moment knelled the woe of years.

34

There they stood, ranged along the hill-sides, met
  To view the last of me, a living frame
  For one more picture! in a sheet of flame
I saw them and I knew them all. And yet
Dauntless the slug-horn to my lips I set,
  And blew. *'Childe Roland to the Dark Tower came.'*

A Grammarian's Funeral

Shortly after the Revival of Learning in Europe

Let us begin and carry up this corpse,
  Singing together.
Leave we the common crofts, the vulgar thorpes
  Each in its tether
Sleeping safe on the bosom of the plain,
  Cared-for till cock-crow:
Look out if yonder be not day again
  Rimming the rock-row!
That's the appropriate country; there, man's thought,
  Rarer, intenser,   10
Self-gathered for an outbreak, as it ought,
  Chafes in the censer.
Leave we the unlettered plain its herd and crop;
  Seek we sepulture
On a tall mountain, citied to the top,
  Crowded with culture!
All the peaks soar, but one the rest excels;
  Clouds overcome it;
No! yonder sparkle is the citadel's
  Circling its summit.   20
Thither our path lies; wind we up the heights:
  Wait ye the warning?
Our low life was the level's and the night's;
  He's for the morning.
Step to a tune, square chests, erect each head,
  'Ware the beholders!
This is our master, famous calm and dead,
  Borne on our shoulders.

Sleep, crop and herd! sleep, darkling thorpe and croft,
                Safe from the weather!   30
He, whom we convoy to his grave aloft,
                Singing together,
He was a man born with thy face and throat,
                Lyric Apollo!
Long he lived nameless: how should spring take note
                Winter would follow?
Till lo, the little touch, and youth was gone!
                Cramped and diminished,
Moaned he, 'New measures, other feet anon!
                'My dance is finished?'   40
No, that's the world's way: (keep the mountain-side,
                Make for the city!)
He knew the signal, and stepped on with pride
                Over men's pity;
Left play for work, and grappled with the world
                Bent on escaping:
'What's in the scroll,' quoth he, 'thou keepest furled?
                'Show me their shaping,
'Theirs who most studied man, the bard and sage,—
                'Give!'—So, he gowned him,   50
Straight got by heart that book to its last page:
                Learned, we found him.
Yea, but we found him bald too, eyes like lead,
                Accents uncertain:
'Time to taste life,' another would have said,
                'Up with the curtain!'
This man said rather, 'Actual life comes next?
                'Patience a moment!
'Grant I have mastered learning's crabbed text,
                'Still there's the comment.   60
'Let me know all! Prate not of most or least,
                'Painful or easy!

'Even to the crumbs I'd fain eat up the feast,
    'Ay, nor feel queasy.'
Oh, such a life as he resolved to live,
    When he had learned it,
When he had gathered all books had to give!
    Sooner, he spurned it.
Image the whole, then execute the parts—
    Fancy the fabric   70
Quite, ere you build, ere steel strike fire from quartz,
    Ere mortar dab brick!

(Here's the town-gate reached: there's the market-place
    Gaping before us.)
Yes, this in him was the peculiar grace
    (Hearten our chorus!)
That before living he'd learn how to live—
    No end to learning:
Earn the means first—God surely will contrive
    Use for our earning.   80
Others mistrust and say, 'But time escapes:
    'Live now or never!'
He said, 'What's time? Leave Now for dogs and apes!
    'Man has Forever.'
Back to his book then: deeper drooped his head:
    Calculus racked him:
Leaden before, his eyes grew dross of lead:
    Tussis attacked him.
'Now, master, take a little rest!'—not he!
    (Caution redoubled,   90
Step two abreast, the way winds narrowly!)
    Not a whit troubled
Back to his studies, fresher than at first,
    Fierce as a dragon
He (soul-hydroptic with a sacred thirst)
    Sucked at the flagon.

Oh, if we draw a circle premature,
      Heedless of far gain,
Greedy for quick returns of profit, sure
        Bad is our bargain!   100
Was it not great? did not he throw on God,
      (He loves the burthen)—
God's task to make the heavenly period
      Perfect the earthen?
Did not he magnify the mind, show clear
      Just what it all meant?
He would not discount life, as fools do here,
      Paid by instalment.
He ventured neck or nothing—heaven's success
      Found, or earth's failure: 110
'Wilt thou trust death or not?' He answered 'Yes:
      'Hence with life's pale lure!'
That low man seeks a little thing to do,
      Sees it and does it:
This high man, with a great thing to pursue,
      Dies ere he knows it.
That low man goes on adding one to one,
      His hundred's soon hit:
This high man, aiming at a million,
      Misses an unit.   120
That, has the world here—should he need the next,
      Let the world mind him!
This, throws himself on God, and unperplexed
      Seeking shall find him.
So, with the throttling hands of death at strife,
      Ground he at grammar;
Still, thro' the rattle, parts of speech were rife:
      While he could stammer
He settled *Hoti's* business—let it be!—
      Properly based *Oun*—   130

Gave us the doctrine of the enclitic *De*,
　　Dead from the waist down.
Well, here's the platform, here's the proper place:
　　Hail to your purlieus,
All ye highfliers of the feathered race,
　　Swallows and curlews!
Here's the top-peak; the multitude below
　　Live, for they can, there:
This man decided not to Live but Know—
　　Bury this man there?　　　　　　　　140
Here—here's his place, where meteors shoot, clouds form,
　　Lightnings are loosened,
Stars come and go! Let joy break with the storm.
　　Peace let the dew send!
Lofty designs must close in like effects:
　　Loftily lying,
Leave him—still loftier than the world suspects,
　　Living and dying.

'Transcendentalism:
A Poem in Twelve Books'

Stop playing, poet! May a brother speak?
'Tis you speak, that's your error. Song's our art:
Whereas you please to speak these naked thoughts
Instead of draping them in sights and sounds.
—True thoughts, good thoughts, thoughts fit to treasure up!
But why such long prolusion and display,
Such turning and adjustment of the harp,
And taking it upon your breast, at length,
Only to speak dry words across its strings?

Stark-naked thought is in request enough: 10
Speak prose and hollo it till Europe hears!
The six-foot Swiss tube, braced about with bark,
Which helps the hunter's voice from Alp to Alp—
Exchange our harp for that,—who hinders you?

But here's your fault; grown men want thought, you think;
Thought's what they mean by verse, and seek in verse.
Boys seek for images and melody,
Men must have reason—so, you aim at men.
Quite otherwise! Objects throng our youth, 'tis true;
We see and hear and do not wonder much: 20
If you could tell us what they mean, indeed!
As German Boehme never cared for plants
Until it happed, a-walking in the fields,
He noticed all at once that plants could speak,
Nay, turned with loosened tongue to talk with him.
That day the daisy had an eye indeed—
Colloquised with the cowslip on such themes!
We find them extant yet in Jacob's prose.
But by the time youth slips a stage or two
While reading prose in that tough book he wrote   30
(Collating and emendating the same
And settling on the sense most to our mind),
We shut the clasps and find life's summer past.
Then, who helps more, pray, to repair our loss—
Another Boehme with a tougher book
And subtler meanings of what roses say,—
Or some stout Mage like him of Halberstadt,
John, who made things Boehme wrote thoughts about?
He with a 'look you!' vents a brace of rhymes,
And in there breaks the sudden rose herself,   40
Over us, under, round us every side,
Nay, in and out the tables and the chairs
And musty volumes, Boehme's book and all,—

Buries us with a glory, young once more,
Pouring heaven into this shut house of life.

So come, the harp back to your heart again!
You are a poem, though your poem's naught.
The best of all you showed before, believe,
Was your own boy-face o'er the finer chords
Bent, following the cherub at the top   50
That points to God with his paired half-moon wings.

How it Strikes a Contemporary

I only knew one poet in my life:
And this, or something like it, was his way.

You saw go up and down Valladolid,
A man of mark, to know next time you saw.
His very serviceable suit of black
Was courtly once and conscientious still,
And many might have worn it, though none did:
The cloak, that somewhat shone and showed the threads,
Had purpose, and the ruff, significance.
He walked and tapped the pavement with his cane,   10
Scenting the world, looking it full in face,
An old dog, bald and blindish, at his heels.
They turned up, now, the alley by the church,
That leads nowhither; now, they breathed themselves
On the main promenade just at the wrong time:
You'd come upon his scrutinising hat,
Making a peaked shade blacker than itself
Against the single window spared some house

Intact yet with its mouldered Moorish work,—
Or else surprise the ferrel of his stick   20
Trying the mortar's temper 'tween the chinks
Of some new shop a-building, French and fine.
He stood and watched the cobbler at his trade,
The man who slices lemons into drink,
The coffee-roaster's brazier, and the boys
That volunteer to help him turn its winch.
He glanced o'er books on stalls with half an eye,
And fly-leaf ballads on the vendor's string,
And broad-edge bold-print posters by the wall.
He took such cognizance of men and things,   30
If any beat a horse, you felt he saw;
If any cursed a woman, he took note;
Yet stared at nobody,—you stared at him,
And found, less to your pleasure than surprise,
He seemed to know you and expect as much.
So, next time that a neighbour's tongue was loosed,
It marked the shameful and notorious fact,
We had among us, not so much a spy,
As a recording chief-inquisitor,
The town's true master if the town but knew!   40
We merely kept a governor for form,
While this man walked about and took account
Of all thought, said and acted, then went home,
And wrote it fully to our Lord the King
Who has an itch to know things, he knows why,
And reads them in his bedroom of a night.
Oh, you might smile! there wanted not a touch,
A tang of . . . well, it was not wholly ease
As back into your mind the man's look came.
Stricken in years a little,—such a brow   50
His eyes had to live under!—clear as flint
On either side the formidable nose
Curved, cut and coloured like an eagle's claw.

83

Had he to do with A.'s surprising fate?
When altogether old B. disappeared
And young C. got his mistress,—was't our friend,
His letter to the King, that did it all?
What paid the bloodless man for so much pains?
Our Lord the King has favourites manifold,
And shifts his ministry some once a month;   60
Our city gets new governors at whiles,—
But never word or sign, that I could hear,
Notified to this man about the streets
The King's approval of those letters conned
The last thing duly at the dead of night.
Did the man love his office? Frowned our Lord,
Exhorting when none heard—'Beseech me not!
'Too far above my people,—beneath me!
'I set the watch,—how should the people know?
'Forget them, keep me all the more in mind!'   70
Was some such understanding 'twixt the two?

    I found no truth in one report at least—
That if you tracked him to his home, down lanes
Beyond the Jewry, and as clean to pace,
You found he ate his supper in a room
Blazing with lights, four Titians on the wall,
And twenty naked girls to change his plate!
Poor man, he lived another kind of life
In that new stuccoed third house by the bridge,
Fresh-painted, rather smart than otherwise!   80
The whole street might o'erlook him as he sat,
Leg crossing leg, one foot on the dog's back,
Playing a decent cribbage with his maid
(Jacynth, you're sure her name was) o'er the cheese
And fruit, three red halves of starved winter-pears,
Or treat of radishes in April. Nine,
Ten, struck the church clock, straight to bed went he.

My father, like the man of sense he was,
Would point him out to me a dozen times;
''St—'St,' he'd whisper, 'the Corregidor!'   90
I had been used to think that personage
Was one with lacquered breeches, lustrous belt,
And feathers like a forest in his hat,
Who blew a trumpet and proclaimed the news,
Announced the bull-fights, gave each church its turn,
And memorised the miracle in vogue!
He had a great observance from us boys;
We were in error; that was not the man.

I'd like now, yet had haply been afraid,
To have just looked, when this man came to die,   100
And seen who lined the clean gay garret-sides
And stood about the neat low truckle-bed,
With the heavenly manner of relieving guard.
Here had been, mark, the general-in-chief,
Thro' a whole campaign of the world's life and death,
Doing the King's work all the dim day long,
In his old coat and up to knees in mud,
Smoked like a herring, dining on a crust,—
And, now the day was won, relieved at once!
No further show or need for that old coat,   110
You are sure, for one thing! Bless us, all the while
How sprucely we are dressed out, you and I!
A second, and the angels alter that.
Well, I could never write a verse,—could you?
Let's to the Prado and make the most of time.

Fra Lippo Lippi

I am poor brother Lippo, by your leave!
You need not clap your torches to my face.
Zooks, what's to blame? you think you see a monk!
What, 'tis past midnight, and you go the rounds,
And here you catch me at an alley's end
Where sportive ladies leave their doors ajar?
The Carmine's my cloister: hunt it up,
Do,—harry out, if you must show your zeal,
Whatever rat, there, haps on his wrong hole,
And nip each softling of a wee white mouse,   10
Weke, weke, that's crept to keep him company!
Aha, you know your betters! Then, you'll take
Your hand away that's fiddling on my throat,
And please to know me likewise. Who am I?
Why, one, sir, who is lodging with a friend
Three streets off—he's a certain . . . how d'ye call?
Master—a . . . Cosimo of the Medici,
I' the house that caps the corner. Boh! you were best!
Remember and tell me, the day you're hanged,
How you affected such a gullet's-gripe!   20
But you, sir, it concerns you that your knaves
Pick up a manner nor discredit you:
Zooks, are we pilchards, that they sweep the streets
And count fair prize what comes into their net?
He's Judas to a title, that man is!
Just such a face! Why, sir, you make amends.
Lord, I'm not angry! Bid your hangdogs go
Drink out this quarter-florin to the health
Of the munificent House that harbours me
(And many more beside, lads! more beside!)   30

And all's come square again. I'd like his face—
His, elbowing on his comrade in the door
With the pike and lantern,—for the slave that holds
John Baptist's head a-dangle by the hair
With one hand ('Look you, now,' as who should say)
And his weapon in the other, yet unwiped!
It's not your chance to have a bit of chalk,
A wood-coal or the like? or you should see!
Yes, I'm the painter, since you style me so.
What, brother Lippo's doings, up and down,   40
You know them and they take you? like enough!
I saw the proper twinkle in your eye—
'Tell you, I liked your looks at very first.
Let's sit and set things straight now, hip to haunch.
Here's spring come, and the nights one makes up bands
To roam the town and sing out carnival,
And I've been three weeks shut within my mew,
A-painting for the great man, saints and saints
And saints again. I could not paint all night—
Ouf! I leaned out of window for fresh air.   50
There came a hurry of feet and little feet,
A sweep of lute-strings, laughs, and whiffs of song,—
Flower o' the broom,
Take away love, and our earth is a tomb!
Flower o' the quince,
I let Lisa go, and what good in life since?
Flower o' the thyme—and so on. Round they went.
Scarce had they turned the corner when a titter
Like the skipping of rabbits by moonlight,—three slim shapes,
And a face that looked up . . zooks, sir, flesh and blood, 60
That's all I'm made of! Into shreds it went,
Curtain and counterpane and coverlet,
All the bed-furniture—a dozen knots,
There was a ladder! Down I let myself,
Hands and feet, scrambling somehow, and so dropped,

And after them. I came up with the fun
Hard by Saint Laurence, hail fellow, well met,—
Flower o' the rose,
If I've been merry, what matter who knows?
And so as I was stealing back again 70
To get to bed and have a bit of sleep
Ere I rise up to-morrow and go work
On Jerome knocking at his poor old breast
With his great round stone to subdue the flesh,
You snap me of the sudden. Ah, I see!
Though your eye twinkles still, you shake your head—
Mine's shaved—a monk, you say—the sting's in that!
If Master Cosimo announced himself,
Mum's the word naturally; but a monk!
Come, what am I a beast for? tell us, now! 80
I was a baby when my mother died
And father died and left me in the street.
I starved there, God knows how, a year or two
On fig-skins, melon-parings, rinds and shucks,
Refuse and rubbish. One fine frosty day,
My stomach being empty as your hat,
The wind doubled me up and down I went.
Old Aunt Lapaccia trussed me with one hand,
(Its fellow was a stinger as I knew)
And so along the wall, over the bridge, 90
By the straight cut to the convent. Six words there,
While I stood munching my first bread that month:
'So, boy, you're minded,' quoth the good fat father
Wiping his own mouth, 'twas refection-time,—
'To quit this very miserable world?
'Will you renounce' . . . 'the mouthful of bread?' thought I;
By no means! Brief, they made a monk of me;
I did renounce the world, its pride and greed,
Palace, farm, villa, shop and banking-house,
Trash, such as these poor devils of Medici 100

Have given their hearts to—all at eight years old.
Well, sir, I found in time, you may be sure,
'Twas not for nothing—the good bellyful,
The warm serge and the rope that goes all round,
And day-long blessed idleness beside!
'Let's see what the urchin's fit for'—that came next.
Not overmuch their way, I must confess.
Such a to-do! They tried me with their books:
Lord, they'd have taught me Latin in pure waste!
Flower o' the clove,   110
All the Latin I construe is, 'amo' I love!
But, mind you, when a boy starves in the streets
Eight years together, as my fortune was,
Watching folk's faces to know who will fling
The bit of half-stripped grape-bunch he desires,
And who will curse or kick him for his pains,—
Which gentleman processional and fine,
Holding a candle to the Sacrament,
Will wink and let him lift a plate and catch
The droppings of the wax to sell again,   120
Or holla for the Eight and have him whipped,—
How say I?—nay, which dog bites, which lets drop
His bone from the heap of offal in the street,—
Why, soul and sense of him grow sharp alike,
He learns the look of things, and none the less
For admonition from the hunger-pinch.
I had a store of such remarks, be sure,
Which, after I found leisure, turned to use.
I drew men's faces on my copy-books,
Scrawled them within the antiphonary's marge,   130
Joined legs and arms to the long music-notes,
Found eyes and nose and chin for A's and B's,
And made a string of pictures of the world
Betwixt the ins and outs of verb and noun,
On the wall, the bench, the door. The monks looked black.

'Nay,' quoth the Prior, 'turn him out, d'ye say?
'In no wise. Lose a crow and catch a lark.
'What if at last we get our man of parts,
'We Carmelites, like those Camaldolese
'And Preaching Friars, to do our church up fine   140
'And put the front on it that ought to be!'
And hereupon he bade me daub away.
Thank you! my head being crammed, the walls a blank,
Never was such prompt disemburdening.
First, every sort of monk, the black and white,
I drew them, fat and lean: then, folk at church,
From good old gossips waiting to confess
Their cribs of barrel-droppings, candle-ends,—
To the breathless fellow at the altar-foot,
Fresh from his murder, safe and sitting there   150
With the little children round him in a row
Of admiration, half for his beard and half
For that white anger of his victim's son
Shaking a fist at him with one fierce arm,
Signing himself with the other because of Christ
(Whose sad face on the cross sees only this
After the passion of a thousand years)
Till some poor girl, her apron o'er her head,
(Which the intense eyes looked through) came at eve
On tiptoe, said a word, dropped in a loaf,   160
Her pair of earrings and a bunch of flowers
(The brute took growling), prayed, and so was gone.
I painted all, then cried ''Tis ask and have;
'Choose, for more's ready!'—laid the ladder flat,
And showed my covered bit of cloister-wall.
The monks closed in a circle and praised loud
Till checked, taught what to see and not to see,
Being simple bodies,—'That's the very man!
'Look at the boy who stoops to pat the dog!
'That woman's like the Prior's niece who comes   170

'To care about his asthma: it's the life!'
But there my triumph's straw-fire flared and funked;
Their betters took their turn to see and say:
The Prior and the learned pulled a face
And stopped all that in no time. 'How? what's here?
'Quite from the mark of painting, bless us all!
'Faces, arms, legs and bodies like the true
'As much as pea and pea! it's devil's-game!
'Your business is not to catch men with show,
'With homage to the perishable clay,   180
'But lift them over it, ignore it all,
'Make them forget there's such a thing as flesh.
'Your business is to paint the souls of men—
'Man's soul, and it's a fire, smoke . . . no, it's not . . .
'It's vapour done up like a new-born babe—
'(In that shape when you die it leaves your mouth)
'It's . . . well, what matters talking, it's the soul!
'Give us no more of body than shows soul!
'Here's Giotto, with his Saint a-praising God,
'That sets us praising,—why not stop with him?   190
'Why put all thoughts of praise out of our head
'With wonder at lines, colours, and what not?
'Paint the soul, never mind the legs and arms!
'Rub all out, try at it a second time.
'Oh, that white smallish female with the breasts,
'She's just my niece . . . Herodias, I would say,—
'Who went and danced and got men's heads cut off!
'Have it all out!' Now, is this sense, I ask?
A fine way to paint soul, by painting body
So ill, the eye can't stop there, must go further   200
And can't fare worse! Thus, yellow does for white
When what you put for yellow's simply black,
And any sort of meaning looks intense
When all beside itself means and looks nought.
Why can't a painter lift each foot in turn,

Left foot and right foot, go a double step,
Make his flesh liker and his soul more like,
Both in their order? Take the prettiest face,
The Prior's niece . . . patron-saint—is it so pretty
You can't discover if it means hope, fear,   215
Sorrow or joy? won't beauty go with these?
Suppose I've made her eyes all right and blue,
Can't I take breath and try to add life's flash,
And then add soul and heighten them threefold?
Or say there's beauty with no soul at all—
(I never saw it—put the case the same—)
If you get simple beauty and nought else,
You get about the best thing God invents:
That's somewhat: and you'll find the soul you have missed,
Within yourself, when you return him thanks.   220
'Rub all out!' Well, well, there's my life, in short,
And so the thing has gone on ever since.
I'm grown a man no doubt, I've broken bounds:
You should not take a fellow eight years old
And make him swear to never kiss the girls.
I'm my own master, paint now as I please—
Having a friend, you see, in the Corner-house!
Lord, it's fast holding by the rings in front—
Those great rings serve more purposes than just
To plant a flag in, or tie up a horse!   230
And yet the old schooling sticks, the old grave eyes
Are peeping o'er my shoulder as I work,
The heads shake still—'It's art's decline, my son!
'You're not of the true painters, great and old;
'Brother Angelico's the man, you'll find;
'Brother Lorenzo stands his single peer:
'Fag on at flesh, you'll never make the third!'
Flower o' the pine,
You keep your mistr . . . manners, and I'll stick to mine!
I'm not the third, then: bless us, they must know!   240

Don't you think they're the likeliest to know,
They with their Latin? So, I swallow my rage,
Clench my teeth, suck my lips in tight, and paint
To please them—sometimes do and sometimes don't;
For, doing most, there's pretty sure to come
A turn, some warm eve finds me at my saints—
A laugh, a cry, the business of the world—
(*Flower o' the peach,*
Death for us all, and his own life for each!)
And my whole soul revolves, the cup runs over,   250
The world and life's too big to pass for a dream,
And I do these wild things in sheer despite,
And play the fooleries you catch me at,
In pure rage! The old mill-horse, out at grass
After hard years, throws up his stiff heels so,
Although the miller does not preach to him
The only good of grass is to make chaff.
What would men have? Do they like grass or no—
May they or mayn't they? all I want's the thing
Settled for ever one way. As it is,   260
You tell too many lies and hurt yourself:
You don't like what you only like too much,
You do like what, if given you at your word
You find abundantly detestable.
For me, I think I speak as I was taught;
I always see the garden and God there
A-making man's wife: and, my lesson learned,
The value and significance of flesh,
I can't unlearn ten minutes afterwards,

You understand me: I'm a beast, I know,   270
But see, now—why, I see as certainly
As that the morning-star's about to shine,
What will hap some day. We've a youngster here
Comes to our convent, studies what I do,

Slouches and stares and let's no atom drop:
His name is Guidi—he'll not mind the monks—
They call him Hulking Tom, he lets them talk—
He picks my practice up—he'll paint apace,
I hope so—though I never live so long,
I know what's sure to follow. You be judge!   280
You speak no Latin more than I, belike;
However, you're my man, you've seen the world
—The beauty and the wonder and the power,
The shapes of things, their colours, lights and shades,
Changes, surprises,—and God made it all!
—For what? Do you feel thankful, ay or no,
For this fair town's face, yonder river's line,
The mountain round it and the sky above,
Much more the figures of man, woman, child,
These are the frame to? What's it all about?   290
To be passed over, despised? or dwelt upon,
Wondered at? oh, this last of course!—you say.
But why not do as well as say,—paint these
Just as they are, careless what comes of it?
God's works—paint anyone, and count it crime
To let a truth slip. Don't object, 'His works
'Are here already; nature is complete:
'Suppose you reproduce her—(which you can't)
'There's no advantage! you must beat her, then.'
For, don't you mark? we're made so that we love   300
First when we see them painted, things we have passed
Perhaps a hundred times nor cared to see;
And so they are better, painted—better to us,
Which is the same thing. Art was given for that;
God uses us to help each other so,
Lending our minds out. Have you noticed, now,
Your cullion's hanging face? A bit of chalk,
And trust me but you should, though! How much more,
If I drew higher things with the same truth!

That were to take the Prior's pulpit-place,   310
Interpret God to all of you! Oh, oh,
It makes me mad to see what men shall do
And we in our graves! This world's no blot for us,
Nor blank; it means intensely, and means good:
To find its meaning is my meat and drink.
'Ay, but you don't so instigate to prayer!'
Strikes in the Prior: 'when your meaning's plain
'It does not say to folk—remember matins,
'Or, mind you fast next Friday!' Why, for this
What need of art at all? A skull and bones,   320
Two bits of stick nailed crosswise, or, what's best,
A bell to chime the hour with, does as well.
I painted a Saint Laurence six months since
At Prato, splashed the fresco in fine style:
'How looks my painting, now the scaffold's down?'
I ask a brother: 'Hugely,' he returns—
'Already not one phiz of your three slaves
'Who turn the Deacon off his toasted side,
'But's scratched and prodded to our heart's content,
'The pious people have so eased their own   330
'With coming to say prayers there in a rage:
'We get on fast to see the bricks beneath.
'Expect another job this time next year,
'For pity and religion grow i' the crowd—
'Your painting serves its purpose!' Hang the fools!

—That is—you'll not mistake an idle word
Spoke in a huff by a poor monk, Got wot,
Tasting the air this spicy night which turns
The unaccustomed head like Chianti wine!
Oh, the church knows! don't misreport me, now!   340
It's natural a poor monk out of bounds
Should have his apt word to excuse himself:
And hearken how I plot to make amends.

I have bethought me: I shall paint a piece
. . . There's for you! Give me six months, then go, see
Something in Sant' Ambrogio's! Bless the nuns!
They want a cast o' my office. I shall paint
God in the midst, Madonna and her babe,
Ringed by a bowery flowery angel-brood,
Lilies and vestments and white faces, sweet   350
As puff on puff of grated orris-root
When ladies crowd to Church at midsummer.
And then i' the front, of course a saint or two—
Saint John, because he saves the Florentines,
Saint Ambrose, who puts down in black and white
The convent's friends and gives them a long day,
And Job, I must have him there past mistake,
The man of Uz (and Us without the z,
Painters who need his patience). Well, all these
Secured at their devotion, up shall come   360
Out of a corner when you least expect,
As one by a dark stair into a great light,
Music and talking, who but Lippo! I!—
Mazed, motionless and moonstruck—I'm the man!
Back I shrink—what is this I see and hear?
I, caught up with my monk's-things by mistake,
My old serge gown and rope that goes all round,
I, in this presence, this pure company!
Where's a hole, where's a corner for escape?
Then steps a sweet angelic slip of a thing   370
Forward, puts out a soft palm—'Not so fast!'
—Addresses the celestial presence, 'nay—
'He made you and devised you, after all,
'Though he's none of you! Could Saint John there draw—
'His camel-hair make up a painting-brush?
'We come to brother Lippo for all that,
'*Iste perfecit opus!*' So, all smile—
I shuffle sideways with my blushing face

Under the cover of a hundred wings
Thrown like a spread of kirtles when you're gay   380
And play hot cockles, all the doors being shut,
Till, wholly unexpected, in there pops
The hothead husband! Thus I scuttle off
To some safe bench behind, not letting go
The palm of her, the little lily thing
That spoke the good word for me in the nick,
Like the Prior's niece . . . Saint Lucy, I would say.
And so all's saved for me, and for the church
A pretty picture gained. Go, six months hence!
Your hand, sir, and good-bye: no lights, no lights!   390
The street's hushed, and I know my own way back,
Don't fear me! There's the grey beginning. Zooks!

Andrea Del Sarto

(Called 'the Faultless Painter')

But do not let us quarrel any more,
No, my Lucrezia; bear with me for once:
Sit down and all shall happen as you wish.
You turn your face, but does it bring your heart?
I'll work then for your friend's friend, never fear,
Treat his own subject after his own way,
Fix his own time, accept too his own price,
And shut the money into this small hand
When next it takes mine. Will it? tenderly?
Oh, I'll content him,—but to-morrow, Love!   10
I often am much wearier than you think,
This evening more than usual, and it seems
As if—forgive now—should you let me sit
Here by the window with your hand in mine

And look a half-hour forth on Fiesole,
Both of one mind, as married people use,
Quietly, quietly the evening through,
I might get up to-morrow to my work
Cheerful and fresh as ever. Let us try.
To-morrow, how you shall be glad for this!   20
Your soft hand is a woman of itself,
And mine the man's bared breast she curls inside.
Don't count the time lost, neither; you must serve
For each of the five pictures we require:
It saves a model. So! keep looking so—
My serpentining beauty, rounds on rounds!
—How could you ever prick those perfect ears,
Even to put the pearl there! oh, so sweet—
My face, my moon, my everybody's moon,
Which everybody looks on and calls his,   30
And, I suppose, is looked on by in turn,
While she looks—no one's: very dear, no less.
You smile? why, there's my picture ready made,
There's what we painters call our harmony!
A common greyness silvers everything,—
All in a twilight, you and I alike
—You, at the point of your first pride in me
(That's gone you know),—but I, at every point;
My youth, my hope, my art, being all toned down
To yonder sober pleasant Fiesole.   40
There's the bell clinking from the chapel-top;
That length of convent-wall across the way
Holds the trees safer, huddled more inside;
The last monk leaves the garden; days decrease,
And autumn grows, autumn in everything.
Eh? the whole seems to fall into a shape
As if I saw alike my work and self
And all that I was born to be and do,
A twilight-piece. Love, we are in God's hand.

How strange now, looks the life he makes us lead;   50
So free we seem, so fettered fast we are!
I feel he laid the fetter: let it lie!
This chamber for example—turn your head—
All that's behind us! You don't understand
Nor care to understand about my art,
But you can hear at least when people speak:
And that cartoon, the second from the door
—It is the thing, Love! so such things should be—
Behold Madonna!—I am bold to say.
I can do with my pencil what I know,   60
What I see, what at bottom of my heart
I wish for, if I ever wish so deep—
Do easily, too—when I say, perfectly,
I do not boast, perhaps: yourself are judge,
Who listened to the Legate's talk last week,
And just as much they used to say in France.
At any rate 'tis easy, all of it!
No sketches first, no studies, that's long past:
I do what many dream of, all their lives,
—Dream? strive to do, and agonise to do,   70
And fail in doing. I could count twenty such
On twice your fingers, and not leave this town,
Who strive—you don't know how the others strive
To paint a little thing like that you smeared
Carelessly passing with your robes afloat,—
Yet do much less, so much less, Someone says,
(I know his name, no matter)—so much less!
Well, less is more, Lucrezia: I am judged.
There burns a truer light of God in them,
In their vexed beating stuffed and stopped-up brain,   80
Heart, or whate'er else, than goes on to prompt
This low-pulsed forthright craftsman's hand of mine.
Their works drop groundward, but themselves, I know,
Reach many a time a heaven that's shut to me,

Enter and take their place there sure enough,
Though they come back and cannot tell the world.
My works are nearer heaven, but I sit here.
The sudden blood of these men! at a word
Praise them, it boils, or blame them, it boils too.
I, painting from myself and to myself,   90
Know what I do, am unmoved by men's blame
Or their praise either. Somebody remarks
Morello's outline there is wrongly traced,
His hue mistaken; what of that? or else,
Rightly traced and well ordered; what of that?
Speak as they please, what does the mountain care?
Ah, but a man's reach should exceed his grasp,
Or what's a heaven for? All is silver-grey
Placid and perfect with my art: the worse!
I know both what I want and what might gain,   100
And yet how profitless to know, to sigh
'Had I been two, another and myself,
'Our head would have o'erlooked the world!' No doubt.
Yonder's a work now, of that famous youth
The Urbinate who died five years ago.
('Tis copied, George Vasari sent it me.)
Well, I can fancy how he did it all,
Pouring his soul, with kings and popes to see,
Reaching, that heaven might so replenish him,
Above and through his art—for it gives way;   110
That arm is wrongly put—and there again—
A fault to pardon in the drawing's lines,
Its body, so to speak: its soul is right,
He means right—that, a child may understand.
Still, what an arm! and I could alter it:
But all the play, the insight and the stretch—
Out of me, out of me! And wherefore out?
Had you enjoined them on me, given me soul,
We might have risen to Rafael, I and you!

Nay, Love, you did give all I asked, I think—   120
More than I merit, yes, by many times.
But had you—oh, with the same perfect brow,
And perfect eyes, and more than perfect mouth,
And the low voice my soul hears, as a bird
The fowler's pipe, and follows to the snare—
Had you, with these the same, but brought a mind!
Some women do so. Had the mouth there urged
'God and the glory! never care for gain.
'The present by the future, what is that?
'Live for fame, side by side with Agnolo!   130
'Rafael is waiting: up to God, all three!'
I might have done it for you. So it seems:
Perhaps not. All is as God over-rules.
Beside, incentives come from the soul's self;
The rest avail not. Why do I need you?
What wife had Rafael, or has Agnolo?
In this world, who can do a thing, will not;
And who would do it, cannot, I perceive:
Yet the will's somewhat—somewhat, too, the power—
And thus we half-men struggle. At the end,   140
God, I conclude, compensates, punishes.
'Tis safer for me, if the award be strict,
That I am something underrated here,
Poor this long while, despised, to speak the truth.
I dared not, do you know, leave home all day,
For fear of chancing on the Paris lords.
The best is when they pass and look aside;
But they speak sometimes; I must bear it all.
Well may they speak! That Francis, that first time,
And that long festal year at Fontainebleau!   150
I surely then could sometimes leave the ground,
Put on the glory, Rafael's daily wear,
In that humane great monarch's golden look,—
One finger in his beard or twisted curl

Over his mouth's good mark that made the smile,
One arm about my shoulder, round my neck,
The jingle of his gold chain in my ear,
I painting proudly with his breath on me,
All his court round him, seeing with his eyes,
Such frank French eyes, and such a fire of souls   160
Profuse, my hand kept plying by those hearts,—
And, best of all, this, this, this face beyond,
This in the background, waiting on my work,
To crown the issue with a last reward!
A good time, was it not, my kingly days?
And had you not grown restless . . . but I know—
'Tis done and past; 'twas right, my instinct said;
Too live the life grew, golden and not grey,
And I'm the weak-eyed bat no sun should tempt
Out of the grange whose four walls make his world.   170
How could it end in any other way?
You called me, and I came home to your heart.
The triumph was—to reach and stay there; since
I reached it ere the triumph, what is lost?
Let my hands frame your face in your hair's gold,
You beautiful Lucrezia that are mine!
'Rafael did this, Andrea painted that;
'The Roman's is the better when you pray,
'But still the other's Virgin was his wife—'
Men will excuse me. I am glad to judge   180
Both pictures in your presence; clearer grows
My better fortune, I resolve to think.
For, do you know, Lucrezia, as God lives,
Said one day Agnolo, his very self,
To Rafael . . . I have known it all these years . . .
(When the young man was flaming out his thoughts
Upon a palace-wall for Rome to see,
Too lifted up in heart because of it)
'Friend, there's a certain sorry little scrub

'Goes up and down our Florence, none cares how,   190
'Who, were he set to plan and execute
'As you are, pricked on by your popes and kings,
'Would bring the sweat into that brow of yours!'
To Rafael's!—And indeed the arm is wrong.
I hardly dare . . . yet, only you to see,
Give the chalk here—quick, thus the line should go!
Ay, but the soul! he's Rafael! rub it out!
Still, all I care for, if he spoke the truth,
What he? why, who but Michel Agnolo?
Do you forget already words like those?)   200
If really there was such a chance, so lost,—
Is, whether you're—not grateful—but more pleased.
Well, let me think so. And you smile indeed!
This hour has been an hour! Another smile?
If you would sit thus by me every night
I should work better, do you comprehend?
I mean that I should earn more, give you more.
See, it is settled dusk now; there's a star;
Morello's gone, the watch-lights show the wall,
The cue-owls speak the name we call them by.   210
Come from the window, love—come in, at last,
Inside the melancholy little house
We built to be so gay with. God is just.
King Francis may forgive me: oft at nights
When I look up from painting, eyes tired out,
The walls become illumined, brick from brick
Distinct, instead of mortar, fierce bright gold,
That gold of his I did cement them with!
Let us but love each other. Must you go?
That Cousin here again! he waits outside?   220
Must see you—you, and not with me? Those loans?
More gaming debts to pay? you smiled for that?
Well, let smiles buy me! have you more to spend?
While hand and eye and something of a heart

Are left me, work's my ware, and what's it worth?
I'll pay my fancy. Only let me sit
The grey remainder of the evening out,
Idle, you call it, and muse perfectly
How could I paint, were I but back in France,
One picture, just one more—the Virgin's face, 230
Not yours this time! I want you at my side
To hear them—that is, Michel Agnolo—
Judge all I do and tell you of its worth.
Will you? To-morrow, satisfy your friend.
I take the subjects for his corridor,
Finish the portrait out of hand—there-there,
And throw him in another thing or two
If he demurs; the whole should prove enough
To pay for this same Cousin's freak. Beside,
What's better and what's all I care about, 240
Get you the thirteen scudi for the ruff!
Love, does that please you? Ah, but what does he,
The Cousin! what does he to please you more?

    I am grown peaceful as old age to-night.
I regret little, I would change still less.
Since there my past life lies, why alter it?
The very wrong to Francis!—it is true
I took his coin, was tempted and complied,
And built this house and sinned, and all is said.
My father and my mother died of want. 250
Well, had I riches of my own? you see
How one gets rich! Let each one bear his lot.
They were born poor, lived poor, and poor they died:
And I have laboured somewhat in my time
And not been paid profusely. Some good son
Paint my two hundred pictures—let him try!
No doubt, there's something strikes a balance. Yes,
You loved me quite enough, it seems to-night.

This must suffice me here. What would one have?
In heaven, perhaps, new chances, one more chance—   260
Four great walls in the New Jerusalem,
Meted on each side by the angel's reed,
For Leonard, Rafael, Agnolo and me
To cover—the three first without a wife,
While I have mine! So—still they overcome
Because there's still Lucrezia,—as I choose.

Again the Cousin's whistle! Go, my Love.

Prospice

Fear death?—to feel the fog in my throat,
    The mist in my face,
When the snows begin, and the blasts denote
    I am nearing the place,
The power of the night, the press of the storm,
    The post of the foe;
Where he stands, the Arch Fear in a visible form,
    Yet the strong man must go:
For the journey is done and the summit attained,
    And the barriers fall,   10
Though a battle's to fight ere the guerdon be gained,
    The reward of it all.
I was ever a fighter, so—one fight more,
    The best and the last!
I would hate that death bandaged my eyes, and forbore,
    And bade me creep past.
No! let me taste the whole of it, fare like my peers
    The heroes of old,
Bear the brunt, in a minute pay glad life's arrears
    Of pain, darkness and cold.   20

For sudden the worst turns the best to the brave,
  The black minute's at end,
And the elements' rage, the fiend-voices that rave,
  Shall dwindle, shall blend,
Shall change, shall become first a peace out of pain,
  Then a light, then thy breast,
O thou soul of my soul! I shall clasp thee again,
  And with God be the rest!

Youth and Art

1

It once might have been, once only:
  We lodged in a street together,
You, a sparrow on the housetop lonely,
  I, a lone she-bird of his feather.

2

Your trade was with sticks and clay,
  You thumbed, thrust, patted and polished,
Then laughed 'They will see some day
  'Smith made, and Gibson demolished.'

3

My business was song, song, song;
  I chirped, cheeped, trilled and twittered,
'Kate Brown's on the boards ere long,
  'And Grisi's existence embittered!'

4

I earned no more by a warble
  Than you by a sketch in plaster;
You wanted a piece of marble,
  I needed a music-master.

We studied hard in our styles,
    Chipped each at a crust like Hindoos,
For air looked out on the tiles,
    For fun watched each other's windows.

You lounged, like a boy of the South,
    Cap and blouse—nay, a bit of beard too;
Or you got it, rubbing your mouth
    With fingers the clay adhered to.

And I—soon managed to find
    Weak points in the flower-fence facing,
Was forced to put up a blind
    And be safe in my corset-lacing.

No harm! It was not my fault
    If you never turned your eye's tail up
As I shook upon E *in alt*,
    Or ran the chromatic scale up:

For spring bade the sparrows pair,
    And the boys and girls gave guesses,
And stalls in our street looked rare
    With bulrush and watercresses.

Why did not you pinch a flower
    In a pellet of clay and fling it?
Why did not I put a power
    Of thanks in a look, or sing it?

11

I did look, sharp as a lynx,
 (And yet the memory rankles)
When models arrived, some minx
 Tripped up stairs, she and her ankles

12

But I think I gave you as good!
 'That foreign fellow,—who can know
'How she pays, in a playful mood,
 'For his tuning her that piano?'

13

Could you say so, and never say
 'Suppose we join hands and fortunes,
'And I fetch her from over the way,
 'Her, piano, and long tunes and short tunes?'

14

No, no: you would not be rash,
 Nor I rasher and something over:
You've to settle yet Gibson's hash,
 And Grisi yet lives in clover.

15

But you meet the Prince at the Board,
 I'm queen myself at *bals-paré*,
I've married a rich old lord,
 And you're dubbed knight and an R.A.

16

Each life unfulfilled, you see;
 It hangs still, patchy and scrappy:
We have not sighed deep, laughed free,
 Starved, feasted, despaired,—been happy.

17

And nobody calls you a dunce,
   And people suppose me clever:
This could but have happened once,
   And we missed it, lost it for ever.

House

1

Shall I sonnet-sing you about myself?
   Do I live in a house you would like to see?
Is it scant of gear, has it store of pelf?
   'Unlock my heart with a sonnet-key?'

2

Invite the world, as my betters have done?
   'Take notice: this building remains on view,
Its suites of reception every one,
   Its private apartment and bedroom too;

3

'For a ticket, apply to the Publisher.'
   No: thanking the public, I must decline.
A peep through my window, if folk prefer;
   But, please you, no foot over threshold of mine!

4

I have mixed with a crowd and heard free talk
   In a foreign land where an earthquake chanced:
And a house stood gaping, nought to baulk
   Man's eye wherever he gazed or glanced.

5

The whole of the frontage shaven sheer,
    The inside gaped: exposed to day,
Right and wrong and common and queer,
    Bare, as the palm of your hand, it lay.

6

The owner? Oh, he had been crushed, no doubt!
    'Odd tables and chairs for a man of wealth!
What a parcel of musty old books about!
    He smoked,—no wonder he lost his health!

7

'I doubt if he bathed before he dressed.
    A brasier?—the pagan, he burned perfumes!
You see it is proved, what the neighbours guessed:
    His wife and himself had separate rooms.'

8

Friends, the goodman of the house at least
    Kept house to himself till an earthquake came:
'Tis the fall of its frontage permits you feast
    On the inside arrangement you praise or blame.

9

Outside should suffice for evidence:
    And whoso desires to penetrate
Deeper, must dive by the spirit-sense—
    No optics like yours, at any rate!

10

'Hoity toity! A street to explore,
    Your house the exception! "*With this same key
Shakespeare unlocked his heart,*" once more!'
    Did Shakespeare? If so, the less Shakespeare he!

Pisgah-Sights. I

1

Over the ball of it.
  Peering and prying,
How I see all of it,
  Life there, outlying!
Roughness and smoothness,
  Shine and defilement,
Grace and uncouthness:
  One reconcilement.

2

Orbed as appointed,
  Sister with brother
Joins, ne'er disjointed
  One from the other.
All's lend-and-borrow;
  Good, see, wants evil,
Joy demands sorrow,
  Angel weds devil!

3

'Which things must—*why* be?'
  Vain our endeavour!
So shall things aye be
  As they were ever.
'Such things should *so* be!'
  Sage our desistence!
Rough-smooth let globe be,
  Mixed—man's existence!

Man—wise and foolish,
    Lover and scorner,
Docile and mulish—
    Keep each his corner!
Honey yet gall of it!
    There's the life lying,
And I see all of it,
    Only, I'm dying!

Pisgah-Sights. II

1

Could I but live again,
    Twice my life over,
Would I once strive again?
    Would not I cover
Quietly all of it—
    Greed and ambition—
So, from the pall of it,
    Pass to fruition?

2

'Soft!' I'd say, 'Soul mine!
    Three-score and ten years,
Let the blind mole mine
    Digging out deniers!
Let the dazed hawk soar,
    Claim the sun's rights too!
Turf 'tis thy walk's o'er,
    Foliage thy flight's to.'

3

Only a learner,
   Quick one or slow one,
Just a discerner,
   I would teach no one.
I am earth's native:
   No rearranging it!
I be creative,
   Chopping and changing it?

4

March, men, my fellows!
   Those who, above me,
(Distance so mellows)
   Fancy you love me:
Those who, below me,
   (Distance makes great so)
Free to forego me,
   Fancy you hate so!

5

Praising, reviling,
   Worst head and best head,
Past me defiling,
   Never arrested,
Wanters, abounders,
   March, in gay mixture,
Men, my surrounders!
   I am the fixture.

6

So shall I fear thee,
    Mightiness yonder!
Mock-sun—more near thee,
    What is to wonder?
So shall I love thee,
    Down in the dark,—lest
Glowworm I prove thee,
    Star that now sparklest!

Fears and Scruples

1

Here's my case. Of old I used to love him
    This same unseen friend, before I knew:
Dream there was none like him, none above him,—
    Wake to hope and trust my dream was true.

2

Loved I not his letters full of beauty?
    Not his actions famous far and wide?
Absent, he would know I vowed him duty;
    Present, he would find me at his side.

3

Pleasant fancy! for I had but letters,
    Only knew of actions by hearsay:
He himself was busied with my betters;
    What of that? My turn must come some day.

'Some day' proving—no day! Here's the puzzle.
    Passed and passed my turn is. Why complain?
He's so busied! If I could but muzzle
    People's foolish mouths that give me pain!

'Letters?' (hear them!) 'You a judge of writing?
    Ask the experts!—How they shake the head
O'er these characters, your friend's inditing—
    Call them forgery from A to Z!

'Actions? Where's your certain proof' (they bother)
    'He, of all you find so great and good,
He, he only, claims this, that, the other
    Action—claimed by men, a multitude?'

I can simply wish I might refute you,
    Wish my friend would,—by a word, a wink,—
Bid me stop that foolish mouth,—you brute you!
    He keeps absent,—why, I cannot think.

Never mind! Though foolishness may flout me,
    One thing's sure enough: 'tis neither frost,
No, nor fire, shall freeze or burn from out me
    Thanks for truth—though falsehood, gained—though lost.

All my days, I'll go the softlier, sadlier,
    For that dream's sake! How forget the thrill
Through and through me as I thought 'The gladlier
    Lives my friend because I love him still!'

Ah, but there's a menace someone utters!
  'What and if your friend at home play tricks?
Peep at hide-and-seek behind the shutters?
  Mean your eyes should pierce through solid bricks?

'What and if he, frowning, wake you, dreamy?
  Lay on you the blame that bricks—conceal?
Say *"At least I saw who did not see me,*
  Does see now, and presently shall feel"?'

'Why, that makes your friend a monster!' say you:
  'Had his house no window? At first nod,
Would you not have hailed him?' Hush, I pray you!
  What if this friend happen to be—God?

Natural Magic

All I can say is—I saw it!
The room was as bare as your hand.
I locked in the swarth little lady,—I swear,
From the head to the foot of her—well, quite as bare!
'No Nautch shall cheat me,' said I, 'taking my stand
At this bolt which I draw!' And this bolt—I withdraw it,
And there laughs the lady, not bare, but embowered
With—who knows what verdure, o'erfruited, o'erflowered?
    Impossible! Only—I saw it!

All I can sing is—I feel it!
This life was as blank as that room;
I let you pass in here. Precaution, indeed?
Walls, ceiling and floor,—not a chance for a weed!
Wide opens the entrance: where's cold now, where's gloom?
No May to sow seed here, no June to reveal it,
Behold you enshrined in these blooms of your bringing,
These fruits of your bearing—nay, birds of your winging!
A fairy-tale! Only—I feel it!

Appearances

And so you found that poor room dull,
    Dark, hardly to your taste, my dear?
Its features seemed unbeautiful:
    But this I know—'twas there, not here,
You plighted troth to me, the word
    Which—ask that poor room how it heard.

And this rich room obtains your praise
    Unqualified,—so bright, so fair,
So all whereat perfection stays?
    Ay, but remember—here, not there,
The other word was spoken! Ask
    This rich room how you dropped the mask!

St. Martin's Summer

1

No protesting, dearest!
  Hardly kisses even!
    Don't we both know how it ends?
How the greenest leaf turns serest,
  Bluest outbreak—blankest heaven,
    Lovers—friends?

2

You would build a mansion,
  I would weave a bower
    —Want the heart for enterprise.
Walls admit of no expansion:
  Trellis-work may haply flower
    Twice the size.

3

What makes glad Life's Winter?
  New buds, old blooms after.
    Sad the sighing 'How suspect
Beams would ere mid-Autumn splinter,
  Rooftree scarce support a rafter,
    Walls lie wrecked?'

4

You are young, my princess!
  I am hardly older:
    Yet—I steal a glance behind.
Dare I tell you what convinces
  Timid me that you, if bolder,
    Bold—are blind?

5

Where we plan our dwelling
  Glooms a graveyard surely!
    Headstone, footstone moss may drape,—
Name, date, violets hide from spelling,—
  But, though corpses rot obscurely,
    Ghosts escape.

6

Ghosts! O breathing Beauty,
  Give my frank word pardon!
    What if I—somehow, somewhere—
Pledged my soul to endless duty
  Many a time and oft? Be hard on
    Love—laid there?

7

Nay, blame grief that's fickle,
  Time that proves a traitor,
    Chance, change, all that purpose warps,—
Death who spares to thrust the sickle
  Laid Love low, through flowers which later
    Shroud the corpse!

8

And you, my winsome lady,
  Whisper with like frankness!
    Lies nothing buried long ago?
Are yon—which shimmer mid the shady
  Where moss and violet run to rankness—
    Tombs or no?

Who taxes you with murder?
  My hands are clean—or nearly!
    Love being mortal needs must pass.
Repentance? Nothing were absurder.
  Enough: we felt Love's loss severely;
    Though now—alas!

Love's corpse lies quiet therefore,
  Only Love's ghost plays truant,
    And warns us have in wholesome awe
Durable mansionry; that's wherefore
  I weave but trellis-work, pursuant
    —Life, to law.

The solid, not the fragile,
  Tempts rain and hail and thunder.
    If bower stand firm at Autumn's close,
Beyond my hope,—why, boughs were agile;
  If bower fall flat, we scarce need wonder
    Wreathing—rose!

So, truce to the protesting,
  So, muffled be the kisses!
    For, would we but avow the truth,
Sober is genuine joy. No jesting!
  Ask else Penelope, Ulysses—
    Old in youth!

For why should ghosts feel angered?
 Let all their interference
  Be faint march-music in the air!
'Up! Join the rear of us the vanguard!
 Up, lovers, dead to all appearance,
  Laggard pair!'

The while you clasp me closer,
 The while I press you deeper,
  As safe we chuckle,—under breath,
Yet all the slyer, the jocoser,—
 'So, life can boast its day, like leap-year,
  Stolen from death!'

Ah me—the sudden terror!
 Hence quick—avaunt, avoid me,
  You cheat, the ghostly flesh-disguised!
Nay, all the ghosts in one! Strange error!
 So, 'twas Death's self that clipped and coyed me,
  Loved—and lied

Ay, dead loves are the potent!
 Like any cloud they used you,
  Mere semblance you, but substance they!
Build we no mansion, weave we no tent!
 Mere flesh—their spirit interfused you!
  Hence, I say!

All theirs, none yours the glamour!
Theirs each low word that won me,
Soft look that found me Love's, and left
What else but you—the tears and clamour
That's all your very own! Undone me—
Ghost-bereft!

Ferishtah's Fancies

Prologue to Ferishtah's Fancies

Pray, Reader, have you eaten ortolans
Ever in Italy?
Recall how cooks there cook them: for my plan's
To—Lyre with Spit ally.
They pluck the birds,—some dozen luscious lumps,
Or more or fewer,—
Then roast them, heads by heads and rumps by rumps,
Stuck on a skewer.
But first,—and here's the point I fain would press,—
Don't think I'm tattling!—   10
They interpose, to curb its lusciousness,
—What, 'twixt each fatling?
First comes plain bread, crisp, brown, a toasted square:
Then, a strong sage-leaf:
(So we find books with flowers dried here and there
Lest leaf engage leaf.)
First, food—then, piquancy—and last of all
Follows the thirdling:
Through wholesome hard, sharp soft, your tooth must bite
Ere reach the birdling.   20

Now, were there only crust to crunch, you'd wince
    Unpalatable!
Sage-leaf is bitter-pungent—so's a quince:
    Eat each who's able!
But through all three bite boldly—lo, the gust!
    Flavour—no fixture—
Flies, permeating flesh and leaf and crust
    In fine admixture.
So with your meal, my poem: masticate
    Sense, sight and song there!   30
Digest these, and I praise your peptics' state,
    Nothing found wrong there.
Whence springs my illustration who can tell?
    —The more surprising
That here eggs, milk, cheese, fruit suffice so well
    For gormandising.
A fancy-freak by contrast born of thee,
    Delightful Gressoney!
Who laughest 'Take what is, trust what may be!
    That's Life's true lesson,—eh?   40

Dubiety

I will be happy if but for once:
    Only help me, Autumn weather,
Me and my cares to screen, ensconce
    In luxury's sofa-lap of leather!

Sleep? Nay, comfort—with just a cloud
    Suffusing day too clear and bright:
Eve's essence, the single drop allowed
    To sully, like milk, Noon's water-white.

Let gauziness shade, not shroud,—adjust,
  Dim and not deaden,—somehow sheathe
Aught sharp in the rough world's busy thrust,
  If it reach me through dreaming's vapour-wreath.

Be life so, all things ever the same!
  For, what has disarmed the world? Outside,
Quiet and peace: inside, nor blame
  Nor want, nor wish whate'er betide.

What is it like that has happened before?
  A dream? No dream, more real by much.
A vision? But fanciful days of yore
  Brought many: mere musing seems not such.

Perhaps but a memory, after all!
  —Of what came once when a woman leant
To feel for my brow where her kiss might fall.
  Truth ever, truth only the excellent!

Now

Out of your whole life give but a moment!
All of your life that has gone before,
All to come after it,—so you ignore,
So you make perfect the present,—condense,
In a rapture of rage, for perfection's endowment,
Thought and feeling and soul and sense—
Merged in a moment which gives me at last
You around me for once, you beneath me, above me—
Me—sure that despite of time future, time past,—
This tick of our life-time's one moment you love me!

How long such suspension may linger? Ah, Sweet—
The moment eternal—just that and no more—
When ecstasy's utmost we clutch at the core
While cheeks burn, arms open, eyes shut and lips meet!

Poetics

'So say the foolish!' Say the foolish so, Love?
   'Flower she is, my rose'—or else 'My very swan is she'—
Or perhaps 'Yon maid-moon, blessing earth below, Love,
   That art thou!'—to them, belike: no such vain words from me.

'Hush rose, blush! no balm like breath,' I chide it:
   'Bend thy neck its best, swan,—hers the whiter curve!'
Be the moon the moon: my Love I place beside it:
   What is she? Her human self—no lower word will serve.

Summum Bonum

All the breath and the bloom of the year in the bag of one bee:
   All the wonder and wealth of the mine in the heart of one
      gem:
In the core of one pearl all the shade and the shine of the sea:
   Breath and bloom, shade and shine,—wonder, wealth, and—
      how far above them—
        Truth, that's brighter than gem,
        Trust, that's purer than pearl,—
Brightest truth, purest trust in the universe—all were for me
      In the kiss of one girl.

A Pearl, A Girl

A simple ring with a single stone
  To the vulgar eye no stone of price:
Whisper the right word, that alone—
  Forth starts a sprite, like fire from ice,
And lo, you are lord (says an Eastern scroll)
Of heaven and earth, lord whole and sole
  Through the power in a pearl.

A woman ('tis I this time that say)
  With little the world counts worthy praise
Utter the true word—out and away
  Escapes her soul: I am wrapt in blaze,
Creation's lord, of heaven and earth
Lord whole and sole—by a minute's birth—
  Through the love in a girl!

Speculative

Others may need new life in Heaven—
  Man, Nature, Art—made new, assume!
Man with new mind old sense to leaven,
  Nature—new light to clear old gloom,
Art that breaks bounds, gets soaring-room.

I shall pray: 'Fugitive as precious—
  Minutes which passed,—return, remain!
Let earth's old life once more enmesh us,
  You with old pleasure, me—old pain,
So we but meet nor part again!'

126

Inapprehensiveness

We two stood simply friend-like side by side,
Viewing a twilight country far and wide,
Till she at length broke silence. 'How it towers
Yonder, the ruin o'er this vale of ours!
The West's faint flare behind it so relieves
Its rugged outline—sight perhaps deceives,
Or I could almost fancy that I see
A branch wave plain—belike some wind-sown tree
Chance-rooted where a missing turret was.
What would I give for the perspective glass   10
At home, to make out if 'tis really so!
Has Ruskin noticed here at Asolo
That certain weed-growths on the ravaged wall
Seem' . . . something that I could not say at all,
My thought being rather—as absorbed she sent
Look onward after look from eyes distent
With longing to reach Heaven's gate left ajar—
'Oh, fancies that might be, oh, facts that are!
What of a wilding? By you stands, and may
So stand unnoticed till the Judgment Day,   20
One who, if once aware that your regard
Claimed what his heart holds,—woke, as from its sward
The flower, the dormant passion, so to speak--
Then what a rush of life would startling wreak
Revenge on your inapprehensive stare
While, from the ruin and the West's faint flare,
You let your eyes meet mine, touch what you term
Quietude—that's an universe in germ—
The dormant passion needing but a look
To burst into immense life!'   'No, the book   30
Which noticed how the wall-growths wave' said she
'Was not by Ruskin.'   I said 'Vernon Lee?'

Epilogue to 'Asolando'

At the midnight in the silence of the sleep-time,
   When you set your fancies free,
Will they pass to where—by death, fools think, imprisoned—
Low he lies who once so loved you, whom you loved so,
        —Pity me?

Oh to love so, be so loved, yet so mistaken!
   What had I on earth to do
With the slothful, with the mawkish, the unmanly?
Like the aimless, helpless, hopeless, did I drivel
      —Being—who?

One who never turned his back but marched breast forward,
   Never doubted clouds would break,
Never dreamed, though right were worsted, wrong would
    triumph,
Held we fall to rise, are baffled to fight better,
       Sleep to wake.

No, at noonday in the bustle of man's work-time
   Greet the unseen with a cheer!
Bid him forward, breast and back as either should be,
'Strive and thrive!' cry 'Speed,—fight on, fare ever
      There as here!'

APPENDIX

(1)

Sun-treader, life and light be thine for ever!
Thou art gone from us; years go by and spring
Gladdens and the young earth is beautiful,
Yet thy songs come not, other bards arise,
But none like thee: they stand, thy majesties,
Like mighty works which tell some spirit there
Hath sat regardless of neglect and scorn,
Till, its long task completed, it hath risen
And left us, never to return, and all
Rush in to peer and praise when all in vain.   10
The air seems bright with thy past presence yet,
But thou art still for me as thou hast been
When I have stood with thee as on a throne
With all thy dim creations gathered round
Like mountains, and I felt of mould like them,
And with them creatures of my own were mixed,
Like things half-lived, catching and giving life.
But thou art still for me who have adored
Tho' single, panting but to hear thy name
Which I believed a spell to me alone,   20
Scarce deeming thou wast as a star to men!
As one should worship long a sacred spring
Scarce worth a moth's flitting, which long grasses cross,
And one small tree embowers droopingly—
Joying to see some wandering insect won
To live in its few rushes, or some locust
To pasture on its boughs, or some wild bird
Stoop for its freshness from the trackless air:
And then should find it but the fountain-head,
Long lost, of some great river washing towns   30
And towers, and seeing old woods which will live

But by its banks untrod of human foot,
Which, when the great sun sinks, lie quivering
In light as some thing lieth half of life
Before God's foot, waiting a wondrous change;
Then pass with reeds which seek to turn or stay
Its course in vain, for it does ever spread
Like a sea's arm as it goes rolling on,
Being the pulse of some great country—so
Wast thou to me, and art thou to the world!   40
And I, perchance, half feel a strange regret
That I am not what I have been to thee:
Like a girl one has silently loved long
In her first loneliness in some retreat,
When, late emerged, all gaze and glow to view
Her fresh eyes and soft hair and lips which bloom
Like a mountain berry: doubtless it is sweet
To see her thus adored, but there have been
Moments when all the world was in our praise,
Sweeter than any pride of after hours.   50
Yet, sun-treader, all hail! From my heart's heart
I bid thee hail! E'en in my wildest dreams,
I proudly feel I would have thrown to dust
The wreaths of fame which seemed o'erhanging me,
To see thee for a moment as thou art.

And if thou livest, if thou lovest, spirit!
Remember me who set this final seal
To wandering thought—that one so pure as thou
Could never die. Remember me who flung
All honour from my soul, yet paused and said   60
'There is one spark of love remaining yet,
'For I have nought in common with him, shapes
'Which followed him avoid me, and foul forms
'Seek me, which ne'er could fasten on his mind;
'And though I feel how low I am to him,
'Yet I aim not even to catch a tone
'Of harmonies he called profusely up;
'So, one gleam still remains, although the last.'
Remember me who praise thee e'en with tears,
For never more shall I walk calm with thee;   70

Thy sweet imaginings are as an air,
A melody some wondrous singer sings,
Which, though it haunt men oft in the still eve,
They dream not to essay; yet it no less
But more is honoured. I was thine in shame,
And now when all thy proud renown is out,
I am a watcher whose eyes have grown dim
With looking for some star which breaks on him
Altered and worn and weak and full of tears.

(2)

I paused again: a change was coming—came:
I was no more a boy, the past was breaking
Before the future and like fever worked.
I thought on my new self, and all my powers
Burst out. I dreamed not of restraint, but gazed
On all things: schemes and systems went and came,
And I was proud (being vainest of the weak)
In wandering o'er thought's world to seek some one
To be my prize, as if you wandered o'er
The White Way for a star.   10

                    And my choice fell
Not so much on a system as a man—
On one, whom praise of mine shall not offend,
Who was as calm as beauty, being such
Unto mankind as thou to me, Pauline,—
Believing in them and devoting all
His soul's strength to their winning back to peace;
Who sent forth hopes and longings for their sake,
Clothed in all passion's melodies: such first
Caught me and set me, slave of a sweet task,   20
To disentangle, gather sense from song:
Since, song-inwoven, lurked there words which seemed
A key to a new world, the muttering
Of angels, something yet unguessed by man.
How my heart leapt as still I sought and found

Much there, I felt my own soul had conceived,
But there living and burning! Soon the orb
Of his conceptions dawned on me; its praise
Lives in the tongues of men, men's brows are high
When his name means a triumph and a pride.
So, my weak voice may well forbear to shame
What seemed decreed my fate: I threw myself
To meet it, I was vowed to liberty,
Men were to be as gods and earth as heaven,
And I—ah, what a life was mine to prove!
My whole soul rose to meet it. Now, Pauline,
I shall go mad, if I recall that time!

NOTES

1. PIPPA'S SONG: THE YEAR'S AT THE SPRING   1841

Pippa Passes, a dramatic poem, was the first of the series *Bells and Pomegranates*. Pippa is the spirit of innocent delight, and as she passes on her way singing, she unconsciously influences others to act for the best.

1. MY LAST DUCHESS   1842

The unnamed Duke of Ferrara, in Lombardy, is bargaining with the Count's envoy about the dowry to be paid by the Count on the proposed marriage of his daughter with the Duke. In censuring his last duchess, whom he has had murdered for no other fault than her instinctive delight in beautiful things and her gratitude to those who gave her them, he unconsciously betrays his own jealous, proud, and greedy nature. The painter, Frà Pandolf, and the sculptor, Claus of Innsbruck, are imaginary.

3. SIBRANDUS SCHAFNABURGENSIS   1844

A lively trifle in the grotesque style, in which Browning contrasts dry-as-dust pedantry with the teeming and multifarious life of nature. The medieval botanical treatise which he dropped for a time in a hollow tree was by a semi-fictional botanist, Sibrandus of Aschafnaburg Characteristic of Browning are his relish for grotesque forms in nature, such as the toadstool and the spider, and his forgiveness towards the old pedant in the final verse.

v.1.   *matin-prime:* early morning.

v.3.   *pont-levis:* drawbridge.

v.4.   *Rabelais:* early sixteenth-century French writer proverbial for coarse and riotous humour.

v.5.   *de profundis, accentibus lætis, cantate!* Sing from the depths with joyful tones!

v.7.   *toused:* rumpled.

     eft: newt.

     right of trover: legal right to possession of chance findings.

v.8.   *John Knox:* sixteenth-century Scottish preacher noted for severity of his moral views.

v.9.   *sufficit:* it is enough.

In later life Browning admitted this portrait was inspired by Words-worth, but having by that time become respectable himself, he was inclined to deny the literal accuracy of the portrait. It is that of a man revered as a liberal, almost a revolutionary, by the younger generation, and deserting them for official rewards (the 'riband' and the 'silver'). Wordsworth accepted the appointment of Poet Laureate in 1843, but for some time before that he had shown conservative sympathies. Notice the suggestion of divine forgiveness in the final line.

7.   THE LOST MISTRESS   1845
v.2.   The red turns grey. Notice the symbolism comparing the change of colour in the vine leaf to the cooling of passion.

8.   MEETING AT NIGHT   1845

8.   PARTING AT MORNING   1845
And straight was a path of gold . . .: the sun had to follow his narrow path of gold, just as I had to pursue my way in the world.

9.   SONG (NAY BUT YOU, WHO DO NOT LOVE HER)   1845

9.   HOME-THOUGHTS, FROM ABROAD   1845

10.   HOME-THOUGHTS, FROM THE SEA   1845
Written as he first sailed into the Mediterranean on his first journey to Venice in 1838. Cape St. Vincent, Cadiz and Trafalgar were all places on the coast of the Iberian Peninsula associated with the main-tenance of English sea-power from the time of Raleigh to that of Nelson.
Jove's planet: Jupiter.

11.   THE ENGLISHMAN IN ITALY   1845
Browning tells the child Fortù, cowering against him for protection against the sirocco, of the things he has noticed in the countryside of Southern Italy. The poem, besides being a successful example of the easy, colloquial style which is one of Browning's most original con-tributions to poetry, is full of vivid sensuous imagery of almost Keatsian richness. He refers to the activities of the peasants, such as the trampling of the wine grapes and the catching of quails in nets, as well as to many foods, fruits and plants unknown in England. 'Trifles', says Fortù at

the end: but Browning suggests that such trifles are all the more precious to him, coming as he does from a country whose main preoccupation is with the solemn Corn Law controversy.

Sirocco: hot moist wind blowing from Africa.

frails: baskets for drying fruit.

lasagne: a kind of macaroni.

sorbs: the sorb-apple, fruit of the service-tree.

fume-weed: the herb fumitory.

lentisks: the mastic-tree.

abbot's own cheek: the hanging, pouch-like cheek of the hog suggests the jowl of a well-fed abbot.

Bellini, Auber: early nineteenth-century operatic composers.

---

20. THE BISHOP ORDERS HIS TOMB AT ST. PRAXED'S CHURCH   1845

In this portrait of an imaginary Bishop, Browning characterises the worldliness and sensuality of a certain type of Renaissance churchman. He portrays the jealousy and covetousness which are scarcely disguised by religious professions.

St. Praxed's Church: an old church in Rome.

l.2. Anselm: the Bishop's son.

l.5. Gandolf: another imaginary churchman.

l.25. basalt: a dark green or black rock.

l.26. tabernacle: stone canopy.

l.31. onion-stone: green and white marble of inferior quality.

l.41. olive-frail: basket for gathering or storing olives.

l.42. lapis lazuli: bright blue stone used in decoration.

l.46. Frascati: village on the hills near Rome.

l.57. Pans and Nymphs: notice the combination of pagan and Christian elements characteristic of Renaissance decorative art.

l.58. tripod: bronze altar at Delphi in ancient Greece.

thyrsus: ornamental staff carried by followers of Bacchus.

l.64. Ah, ye hope to revel . . . : You were hoping to waste my wealth in revelry while my body decays in a pauper's tomb of *travertine* (mere limestone).

l.77. Tully: Cicero, considered the master of Latin prose in classical times.

l.79. Ulpian: a later Latin writer considered very inferior to Cicero.

l.89. mortcloth: pall.

l.95. St. Praxed at his sermon on the mount: St. Praxed was a woman. The Bishop is becoming confused.

l.99. *elucescebat:* the Bishop is laughing at the bad Latin of his rival, Gandolf's, inscription.

l.106. *Or ye would heighten . . . :* the Bishop imagines his sons in their ingratitude executing his tomb, not as he had ordered, but with insulting additions in the decoration.

l.115. *Term:* a bust ending in a square block of stone, like those of the god Terminus.

24. A WOMAN'S LAST WORD   1855

Let us argue no more, the woman pleads, lest the search for truth end our happiness. Although she knows that her submission of spirit will cause her some regret, she gives in to him for the sake of harmony, and in this sense she has the 'last word'.

26. LOVE AMONG THE RUINS   1855

Browning contrasts the reality of love with the transience of worldly glory.

29. A LOVERS' QUARREL   1855

The weather is perfect, but the lovers have quarrelled. She has left him, and he had rather it were the bitter weather in which they first met, for he cannot enjoy nature without her. Three months ago love made them secure against bad weather; idle diversions made them happy. They were like two people in a dream, sleeping as the earth sleeps under the spell of snow: how could they have any sense of insecurity? How were they to know that the devil of disagreement would pierce to the centre of their happiness and make her his enemy? It was a mere word that offended her, coming only from the lips and not the heart. He begs her not to let 'a moment's spite' make her cast him off for ever. The world's praise or blame is of no importance, but he cannot bear to be misunderstood in 'the one thing rare', his love. Spring is approaching; if only November were here—then in adversity the lovers would find the mutual dependence which they did not feel in summer. In winter weather she would forgive him, and they would be reunited.

v.2. *beryl:* a precious stone of pale blue-green colour. The word is used to suggest the colour of the stream's bed.

v.18. *We shall have the word. . . .:* the cuckoo will announce spring in the minor third of its peculiar notes. This is an example of Browning's fondness for musical terms.

An excellent example of Browning's colloquial writing at its most lively and fluent. Although the speaker is an impoverished Italian gentleman, in his love of the teeming and garish life of the city, he is to some extent the spokesman of Browning's own sentiments.

v.8. cicala: a shrill, chirping insect something like a grasshopper.

v.9. Pulcinello trumpet: trumpet announcing arrival of travelling players, among whom would be Pulcinello, or Punch, the traditional clown.

a sonnet . . . : a fulsome effusion to some divine whose recent sermons challenged even those of St. Paul himself, and who is compared to the early Italian poets and the fathers of the Church.

seven swords: symbolic of the seven sorrows of Mary.

v.10. what oil pays . . . : the tax imposed on farm produce brought into the city.

38. A TOCCATA OF GALUPPI'S   1855

Baldassare Galuppi was an eighteenth-century Venetian composer and musician. A toccata is a piece of music for a keyboard instrument, intended to show off dexterity of touch; it has a lively rhythm which Browning here imitates. Browning imagines himself hearing this composition, which calls up the vain, frivolous life of eighteenth-century Venice; a pair of lovers break off their conversation to listen to the master with an air of condescension. They and all they stood for have long been extinct. As Browning meditates on their fate, he imagines the dead composer passing severe judgment on his Venetian contemporaries; and yet, he thinks, among these foolish, worldly people there had after all been beauty, charm and the warmth of life; he has not the heart to condemn, and suddenly feels old and chilly. This note of forgiveness is characteristic.

v.2. St. Mark's: the Cathedral, where Galuppi was in charge of the music.

the Doges: every year the Doge (chief magistrate) performed a symbolic marriage ceremony with the sea (indicative of the sea-power of the Venetian Republic) by dropping a ring over the side of his state barge.

v.3. Shylock's bridge: the Rialto.

it's as if I saw it all: Galuppi's music calls up a picture of Venetian life.

v.6. clavichord: Browning possibly means harpsichord, of which

Galuppi was a celebrated player. The clavichord is also a keyboard instrument popular at this time.

v.7. In this and the next two verses Browning interprets some imaginary musical passages in terms of human feelings. *Lesser* (minor) *thirds, diminished sixths, suspensions, solutions, the dominant, octave:* all these are harmonic effects suggestive of the moods Browning attributes to them.

v.8. A lovers' dialogue suggested by the music. Perhaps one of the couple is getting tired of the affair.

v.12–14. The dead Galuppi tells Browning how the fops and coquettes of his Venice were, like butterflies, doomed to extinction (*dust and ashes*), while no doubt he (the poet) with his knowledge of science would never die.

v.15. And yet, Browning concludes, were they not beautiful, and do not I, in spite of all my knowledge and philosophy, lack youth and warmth?

gold: Venetian ladies were noted for their auburn hair.

41. 'DE GUSTIBUS——'   1855

The complete proverb is 'De gustibus non disputandum'—'There is no disputing about tastes'.

v.2.   *Cicala:* a chirping insect like a grasshopper.

the king: Ferdinand II of Naples, nicknamed Bomba, was a noted tyrant of Bourbon descent. Here Browning shows his sympathy with the Republican cause in Italy.

Open my heart . . . : these two lines were inscribed on a commemorative tablet placed on the house in Venice where Browning died in 1889.

43. BY THE FIRESIDE   1855

Browning traces the story of his courtship of Elizabeth in terms of a landscape which is at once a familiar Italian scene and a symbolic picture. A characteristic idea recurs—that of the vital moment which makes a man's life, for better or worse.

v.6.   He thinks of Italy as a feminine country.

v.21–22. Addressed directly to his wife (disguised as *Leonore*). *The path grey heads abhor:* the path to death. *The crag's sheer edge:* death itself.

v.23. A portrait of his wife.

v.27.   *the great Word:* Death.

the House not made with hands: the grave.

*v.*30.   *Break the rosary* . . . : take our past life to pieces and examine the separate incidents.

*v.*37.   *chrysolite:* a precious stone of greenish-gold colour.

*v.*46.   *a shadowy third* . . . : if a man and wife are imperfectly united, there is always near them the shadowy figure of the ideal unity they might have achieved.

*v.*51.   Perhaps the clearest statement Browning ever made of his considered view of his own life.

54.   TWO IN THE CAMPAGNA   1855

Here Browning writes of the sense of division which at times saddens the thoughts of any lover. The scene is the Campagna, the open space round Rome, dotted with ruins and covered with flowers in spring. This is another of Browning's symbolic landscapes. The thought he is trying to express is likened to the spider's gossamer thread, blown hither and thither and impossible to grasp.

56.   MISCONCEPTIONS   1855

The two verses are parallel statements of the same theme. The spray on which the bird sang for a while before departing for the treetop where it made its permanent nest imagined, in a sort of pathetic fallacy, that the bird had come there to stay. This was the spray's misconception. The lover's misconception was that the Queen's passing fancy for him was permanent.

*v.*2.   *dalmatic:* a priestly robe worn by those of high dignity and worth.

57.   MEMORABILIA   1855
(*Memorabilia:* Latin for 'Memorable things')

Here again Browning uses nature to symbolise a human idea. The man he is addressing is a commonplace person, to whom a meeting with Shelley was nothing out of the ordinary. Shelley was Browning's great inspiration in poetry, and to have actually seen him would have been to him an event as marvellous and memorable as to pick up an eagle's feather on a stretch of barren moorland. The last line implies: Well, I won't go on, as you wouldn't understand.

58.   POPULARITY   1855

A poem about popular poetry, somewhat difficult to follow in all its details.

v.1–2. I will portray the poet before he leaves us and achieves immortality. Why does God lead him safely through the sorrows of the world unless for some special purpose?

v.3–4. God will one day reveal all the beauty of the world. Until then the poet exists to interpret it for future generations. On that final day, whoever is spokesman for mankind will raise his glass and acknowledge the surpassing quality of God's gift of essential beauty.

v.5–10. Meanwhile, I will draw the poet as he exists amidst the world's indifference, likening him to a fisher on the shores of Tyre. He brings to land the apparently insignificant shell-fish (the murex) from which the wonderful blue Tyrian dye is made, used by the Phœnicians to dye their silks the colour of their goddess Astarte's eyes. The bystanders, like the literary critics, would compare his find with the great prizes of the past. Yet there is the dye—enough to furnish hangings for Solomon's temple, so that the king on his gold throne would be like the golden spike in the centre of the bluebell.

v. 11–12. But (Browning continues ironically) the poet's original intuitions, like the shell-fish, are mere raw material until his imitators, like the manufacturers of dye, come to popularise them; and then, in the products of the imitators (Hobbs, Nobbs, etc.) the poet's discoveries are made cheap and saleable.

v.13. While these poetasters feed on claret and turtle soup, it is forgotten who had the original inspiration which is diluted in their poems, and that the true poet—the Keats—ate poorly in order to make them rich.

61. A LIGHT WOMAN 1855

An interesting example of Browning's ingenuity in dramatisation: it is not made clear until the final verse that Browning imagines himself as the hearer, not the speaker. Of this poem Mrs. Orr, Browning's first biographer, wrote in 1885:

'A man desires to extricate his friend from the toils of "a light woman"; and to this end he courts her himself. He is older and more renowned than her present victim, and trusts to her vanity to ensure his success. But his attentions arouse in her something more. He discovers too late that he has won her heart. He can only cast it away, and a question therefore arises: he knows how it appears to his friend; he knows how he will appear to the woman whom his friend loved; "how does he appear to himself?" In other words, did the end for which he has acted justify the means employed? He doubts it.'

v.7. *basilisk:* fabulous reptile capable of killing with a look.

The lover has failed, but he accepts his failure with resignation. He believes that life is more important than art, and that to strive is the most important thing in life. Public success is nothing compared with the effort to live fully. The only thing that matters to him is that his mistress has consented to this last ride, which he imagines as going on for ever.

v.6. they scratch his name . . . : he is given a memorial in Westminster Abbey.

67. 'CHILDE ROLAND TO THE DARK TOWER CAME' 1855

This has long been regarded as one of Browning's most striking poems, but there has been little agreement as to its significance. G. K. Chesterton, for instance, said: 'What does the poem of *Childe Roland* mean? The only genuine answer to this is, "What does anything mean?" Does the earth mean nothing? Do grey skies and wastes covered with thistles mean nothing? Does an old horse turned out to graze mean nothing? If it does, there is but one further truth to be added—that everything means nothing.' This is not very helpful. Mr. Osbert Burdett, though a little more informative, has not much to add: 'One example of . . . the grotesque at its most romantic, is the weirdly beautiful *Childe Roland*. Nothing, in a sense, is less like Browning than this beautiful poem. The romantic horror of landscape has been rendered so faultlessly that romantic readers have searched for an allegory where none was intended.' Mr. J. M. Cohen, in his *Robert Browning* (Longmans, 1952: pp. 77–82), has much to say about the poem, and seems less inclined to dismiss the possibility of allegorical intention: 'There is obvious relevance,' he writes, 'in this situation to Browning's former half-hearted rebellion seen by him still in these same terms of betrayal; his "lying" wish was for a failure which would excuse him from further endeavours, for a collapse like that of the poet of *Pauline*.'

Of the landscape through which Roland rides, Mr. Cohen says: 'He was now riding through a desolate country, symbolising some lesser "dark night of the soul".' And again: 'Browning's frequent return to themes of brutality and melodramatic disgust, his startling use of images repulsive in their physical horror, arose from his deep, though only sporadic, realisation that the soul of unregenerate man presents an extremely ugly picture. His optimism, for which he was so often reproached, lay in his belief that a treasure existed and could be found, by which a man could be saved. Nowhere, indeed, is his imagery so

hideously obsessed as in the description of that country through which
the knight, only half willingly, rode to find that ray of hope which is
not permitted to break until the poem's last verse.' A writer in *The
Times Literary Supplement* (June 4th, 1954) believes wholeheartedly in
the poem's allegorical significance. 'And what is possibly the greatest
of Browning's shorter poems, *Childe Roland to the Dark Tower Came*,
is an allegory of the fallen human condition, the long ride away from
the comparative innocence of childhood and hopefulness of youth,
towards the "moment of truth" or the moment of judgment when we
touch, at last, on our mortal limits.'

Finally, to return to Browning's first biographer, Mrs. Orr, who
had the advantage of knowing the poet personally, it is interesting to
recall in full what she wrote in her handbook of 1885:

'*Childe Roland to the Dark Tower Came* describes a brave knight
performing a pilgrimage, in which hitherto all who attempted it
have failed. The way through which he struggled is unknown to
him; its features are hideous; a deadly sense of difficulty and danger
hangs over every step; and though Childe Roland's courage is
pledged to the undertaking, the thought of failure at last comes to
him as a relief. He reaches the goal just as failure appears inevitable.
The plain has suddenly closed in; weird and unsightly eminences
encompass him on every side. In one flash he perceives that he is in
a trap; in another, the tower stands before him; while round it,
against the hill-sides, are ranged the "lost adventurers" who have
preceded him—their names and story clanging loudly and more
loudly in his ears—their forms revealed with ghastly clearness in the
last fires of the setting sun.

'So far the picture is consistent; but if we look below its surface
discrepancies appear. The Tower is much nearer and more accessible
than Childe Roland has thought; a sinister-looking man, of whom
he asked the way, and who, as he believed, was deceiving him, has
really put him on the right track; and as he describes the country
through which he passes, it becomes clear that half its horrors are
created by his own heated imagination, or by some undefined influ-
ence in the place itself. We are left in doubt whether those who
have found failure in this quest, have not done so through the very
act of attainment in it; and when, dauntless, Childe Roland sounds
his slughorn and announces that he has come, we should not know,
but that he lives to tell the tale, whether in doing this he incurs, or
is escaping, the general doom. We can connect no idea of definite

pursuit or attainment with a series of facts so dreamlike and so disjointed: still less extract from it a definite moral; and we are reduced to taking the poem as a simple work of fancy, built up of picturesque impressions which have, separately or collectively, produced themselves in the author's mind.[1]

'But these picturesque impressions have, also, their ideal side, which Mr. Browning as spontaneously reproduced; and we may all recognise under the semblance of the enchanted country and the adventurous knight, a poetic vision of life: with its conflicts, contradictions, and mockeries; its difficulties which give way when they seem most insuperable; its successes which look like failures, and its failures which look like success. The thing we may not do is to imagine that an intended lesson is conveyed by it.'

Childe: a medieval word for 'Knight'.

*v.*8. *estray:* stray animal.

*v.*11. *calcine:* burn.

*v.*12. *pashing:* beating, stamping.

*v.*14. *colloped:* lacerated.

*v.*23. *cirque:* circular depression resembling an amphitheatre.

*v.*24. *Tophet:* Hell.

*v.*27. *Apollyon:* a monster in The Pilgrim's Progress.

*v.*31. *mocking elf:* Browning is here thinking of Ariel in *The Tempest*, in the form of lightning.

*v.*34. *slug-horn:* a horn used to blow a challenge. Originally the word meant a 'war-cry' or 'slogan'.

76. A GRAMMARIAN'S FUNERAL   1855

A difficult poem to read and comprehend, because of the irregular rhythm, curious rhymes, and strained syntax. All these are, however, deliberate: they suggest the dead grammarian's difficult progress through life, the intractable material of his studies, and the uneven path up the hillside taken by the bearers, his disciples, who carry his body to the burial-place.

Despite the roughness of its surface and its movement, however, the thought of the poem is not obscure. This imaginary Renaissance scholar

[1] 'I may venture to state that these picturesque materials included a tower which Mr. Browning once saw in the Carrara Mountains, a painting which caught his eye years later in Paris; and the figure of a horse in the tapestry in his own drawing-room—welded together in the remembrance of the line from which King Lear forms the heading of the poem.'

has sacrificed worldly success and well-being to the single-minded pursuit of knowledge for its own sake. Life in time means nothing to him, because he believes in immortality. Browning contrasts the worldling, the 'low man' who is content with petty achievements, and 'this high man' who aims beyond his reach and finds his reward only in the next world.

l.3. croft: small-holding attached to cottage.

thorpe: village.

Notice how the landscape, as is usual in Browning, is conceived symbolically: its various phases, as the bearers go on their way, represent phases in the progress of the grammarian, beginning in homely surroundings and ending amidst the lightning and the stars of his lonely eminence.

l.12. Chafes in the censer! i.e. Is anxious to be free. (The exact significance of this phrase is obscure: *censer* evidently means some kind of containing vessel, not necessarily ecclesiastical unless Browning means that thought is a kind of incense offered to God.)

l.13. Leave we the unlettered plain . . . : these four lines indicate Browning's own preference for the human civilisation of cities over uncultured nature.

l.34. Apollo: the Greek God of poetry. It seems that this grammarian had been destined for poetic fame. Browning may be thinking of his own early hopes, and his failure to achieve popularity, which caused him a growing sense of frustration until his eventual recognition.

l.47. 'What's in the scroll,' . . . : i.e. he resolves, through scholarship, to understand the message of the bards and sages.

l.79. God surely will contrive . . . : even if the labours of a grammarian may seem to the world wasted, God will find a use for them.

l.86. Calculus: the stone, an internal disease.

l.88. Tussis: coughing.

l.95. hydroptic: thirsty (for knowledge alone).

l.97. Oh, if we draw a circle . . . : The circle is the symbol of completeness and perfection. If we try to achieve perfection in this world, we do badly; God will perfect our lives hereafter.

l.129–131. Hoti, Oun, and *De:* Greek particles.

l.134. purlieus: haunts.

80. 'TRANSCENDENTALISM: A POEM IN TWELVE BOOKS'   1855

The title is that of an imaginary philosophical poem. Browning is here discussing poetry with an imaginary fellow-poet. The theme of the argument is the question whether poetry should have a message. The age we live in, Browning maintains, prefers the six-foot trumpet of prose to the harp of lyric poetry. (He is probably thinking of Carlyle, Mill, and Ruskin.) The mystic Jacob Boehme wrapped up his intuitions about flowers in the abstract language of philosophy. The lyric writer Johannes Gleim of Halberstadt was the truer poet. It is our intuitions, not our reflections, which are most truly poetic. You were a better poet, he concludes, as a boy absorbed by the lyric harp than you are as a man moralising in verse. Browning is really talking to himself about the dual quality of his own writing.

l.6. prolusion: preamble.

l.22. Jacob Boehme was a German (not Swedish) mystical philosopher of the early seventeenth century.

l.37. mage: magician or prophet.

him of Halberstadt: an early nineteenth-century minor German poet, Johannes Gleim.

l.50. Cherub at the top: i.e. carved decoratively on the harp.

82. HOW IT STRIKES A CONTEMPORARY   1855

Browning's colloquial style at its best. Local atmosphere is admirably suggested by clear-cut details, so that we are vividly aware of a Spanish town in the seventeenth or eighteenth century. The portrait is a realisation of Browning's idea of a poet in his true function, that of a sort of conscience, at once private and social, mediating between the individual and God. The ten lines beginning 'He took such cognizance of men' are especially significant.

l.90. Corregidor: chief magistrate.

l.115. Prado: the fashionable promenade in Madrid.

86. FRA LIPPO LIPPI   1855

Fra (Brother) Filippo Lippi (1412–69), the orphaned son of a butcher, was taken in by the Carmelite Friars in Florence at the age of eight. He was a natural artist, and found the restrictions, both of monastic life and of the medieval view of art, hampering to his genius. In life he did not renounce the world and the flesh; in art he represented the outlook of the early Italian Renaissance. Cosimo dei Medici was his patron, and Botticelli his pupil. It is the Renaissance outlook which Browning here makes him express—namely, that God created the beauty of the world, and that by making men see it in all its wealth and freshness, the artist serves God.

You've seen the world (Lippo says to his companion),
The beauty and the wonder and the power. . . .
        What's it all about?
To be passed o'er, despised? or dwelt upon,
Wondered at? oh, this last of course, you say.
But why not do as well as say,—paint these
Just as they are, careless what comes of it?
God's works—paint any one, and count it crime
To let a truth slip.

Browning put a good deal of himself into this monologue, and states quite clearly his own view of art (in which he would include poetry).

        This world's no blot for us,
    Nor blank—it means intensely, and means good:
    To find its meaning is my meat and drink.

l.7. *Carmine:* i.e. of the order of Carmelites or White Friars.

l.25. *He's Judas:* Lippo with his painter's eye has noticed among the watch a good model for Judas.

l.31. *I'd like his face:* another suggests to him a model for the slave who beheaded John the Baptist.

l.67. *St. Laurence:* Florentine church where Cosimo dei Medici was buried.

l.74. *Jerome:* one of the early Fathers of the Church, and an ascetic.

l.84. *shucks:* husks.

l.121. *the Eight:* i.e. the magistrates.

l.130. *the antiphonary:* a Catholic service book.

l.139. *Camaldolese:* an order of Monks.

l.235. *Brother Angelico:* Fra Angelico (1387–1455), an older painter of more ascetic tendency.

l.236. *Brother Lorenzo:* a still earlier painter of the Camaldolese order.

l.307. *cullion:* rogue.

l.351. *orris-root:* root of an iris used for perfume.

97. ANDREA DEL SARTO 1855

Andrea del Sarto, a Florentine of the early sixteenth century, was known as 'the Perfect Painter' owing to his technical mastery. He married Lucrezia del Fede, whom he loved all his life for her beauty, and used as a model for his Madonnas and other paintings.

He was commissioned by Francis I to decorate his palace of Fontaine-bleau, but Lucrezia tired of the French court and insisted on their return to Florence, where Andrea betrayed his patron's confidence by building a house for Lucrezia with the money he had been given for the purchase of pictures. Lucrezia admired his art for its commercial value, but was indifferent to his love; she was unfaithful, and finally left him. In poverty and disgrace, he died of the plague. Despite his artistic mastery, he showed a certain listlessness of character; as Browning portrays him, he has been content to exploit his technical excellence, but recognises that the striving of other painters to overcome their imperfections entitles them to a higher place than he can claim.

> Ah, but a man's reach should exceed his grasp,
> Or what's a Heaven for?

In short, Browning condemns Andrea because he is not for ever striving towards the unattainable. He is the counterpart of the hero of *A Grammarian's Funeral*.

l.5. your friend's friend: Andrea is to paint a picture for the friend of his wife's lover, and the fee will go to Lucrezia to pay her lover's debts.

l.15. Fiesole: village on the outskirts of Florence.

l.31. And, I suppose, is looked on . . . : the clumsy syntax of this line and the next seem to me unintelligible.

l.35. A common greyness silvers everything: Andrea's paintings are steeped in this colour, which Browning sees as symbolic of his tired, almost insipid outlook.

l.78. less is more: i.e. the inferior productions of other artists are more than mine in God's sight, because they try harder.

l.93. Morello: the Monte Morello, a hill outside Florence.

l.104. The Urbinate: the painter Rafael, born at Urbino.

l.105. George Vasari: a pupil of Andrea del Sarto, and the author of the famous *Lives of the Painters*, from which Browning took his facts.

l.167. Too live the life grew: life at the French court was becoming too lively and vigorous for my habit of mind.

l.176. 'Rafael did this . . .': Andrea imagines people comparing him and Rafael, and saying that although Rafael's Madonna is more spiritual, Andrea at least had his wife for a model.

l.183. Said one day Agnolo: one day the great Michelangelo himself said to Rafael, who was elated over the success of his mural paintings in Rome, 'My friend, there is a miserable-looking little fellow in Florence, who, if he were given your commissions, would make you sweat with envy.' He refers, of course, to Andrea.

l.209. cue-owls: kind of owl common in Italy.

l.240. *scudi:* crowns. Evidently she is to have money to buy herself a ruff with which to adorn herself.

105. PROSPICE   1864

Elizabeth Barrett Browning died in June 1861, and this poem was written a few months later. *Prospice:* Look forward (Latin).

106. YOUTH AND ART   1864

Browning here recaptures something of the lightness of touch and the easy conversational movement of earlier poems in the manner of, say, *Up at a Villa—Down in the City.* He is dealing with a favourite theme, that of lives wasted through lost opportunity. In this case it is the desire for worldly success which has thwarted the impulse towards natural love.

v.2. Smith made and Gibson demolished: Smith is the unknown sculptor himself; John Gibson, who was made an R.A. in 1838, was one of the most celebrated sculptors of the day, and was commissioned to execute a statue of Queen Victoria for the Houses of Parliament.

v.3. Kate Brown's on the boards ere long, And Grisi's existence embittered: the appearance on the stage of Kate Brown, the young singer of the poem, would threaten the position of the great Italian primadonna, Giulia Grisi, one of the greatest opera singers of the day.

v.15. meet the Prince at the Board: meet the Prince Consort at a Board Meeting of the Royal Academy.

     bals-paré: full-dress balls.

109. HOUSE   1876

Browning deprecates public curiosity about a poet's private life.

v.1. Unlock . . . : the reference is to Wordsworth's sonnet on The Sonnet, where he says, 'With this key Shakespeare unlocked his heart'. Later (*v.10*) Browning is sceptical as to whether Shakespeare really revealed himself in his sonnets.

v.9. whoso desires to penetrate . . . : if you want to know more about me, it must be through intuitive understanding of my poems, not vulgar curiosity.

111. PISGAH-SIGHTS: 1   1876

Browning imagines his own view of life in terms of the sight of the promised land given to Moses on the top of Mount Pisgah, after he had led the Israelites out of Egypt. He did not himself enter the promised land—this is referred to in the last line of the poem. Browning actually lived for thirteen years after its publication.

v.1. *the ball of it:* the earth's globe.

v.2. *Orbed as appointed:* moving in their appointed spheres.

v.3. *Sage our desistence:* we would be wise to refrain from protest and accept things as they are.

112. PISGAH-SIGHTS: II   1876

This cryptic poem expresses Browning's acceptance of life as it is. If he could live again, he would be content, he says, not to strive, but to pass without ambition from death to life's final fulfilment. Let other men spend their span of life grubbing for ha'pence or on the other hand seeking fame like the eagle; my soul would be content with the tree-shaded walks of obscurity. I would prefer to be a learner, not a teacher, happy to leave nature unchanged. Let men march on, those above me (the eagles) imagining they love me, those below me (the moles) imagining they hate me, since the view of the one is mellowed by distance, while to the others I appear great: let them pass by, praising or blaming, while I keep my fixed place in the centre. I would have no fear of the world; I would be content to view fame from far below, lest what I thought was a star should prove, on closer examination, to be no more than a glow-worm.

114. FEARS AND SCRUPLES   1876

A characteristically disguised expression of Browning's faith in God, despite the world's scepticism. The title is taken from Banquo's words in *Macbeth* (Act II, Scene III):

> Fears and scruples shake us:
> In the great hand of God I stand, and thence
> Against the undivulg's pretence I fight
> Of treasonous malice.

v.5–6. The poet's other friends cast doubt on the existence of this special, unseen friend. His letters, they say, are forgeries; and how can Browning be certain that this friend alone is responsible for certain acts for which the credit is claimed by men?

v.8 *'tis neither frost . . . .:* nothing shall destroy my thankfulness for truth, even though I should lose by truth and gain by falsehood.

v.10–11. I hear someone murmur threateningly: 'Perhaps your friend is at home playing tricks on you, playing a game of hide-and-seek behind the shutters and expecting you to see him through his brick walls. Suppose he is angry and blames you because his brick walls hide him. Suppose he should say, "At least I made you aware of my presence, which you shall soon feel." '

116. NATURAL MAGIC 1876

Long after his wife's death Browning experienced a feeling of wonder at the transformation she had brought about in his life.

In his shorter lyrics Browning often illustrated his meaning by two parallel statements, e.g. *Misconceptions* (1855).

*v.*1. *Nautch:* East Indian dancer.

117. APPEARANCES 1876

Another example of Browning's fondness for parallelism. There is no reason to suppose that the situation hinted at is anything but fictional.

118. ST. MARTIN'S SUMMER 1876

A man is speaking to a woman: love between them is dead. She has killed it by trying to base it on too solid a foundation—she has tried to enclose it in a house. He wants to revive love on a less solid but more lasting basis, a bower, which leaves room for change and growth. He wants a St. Martin's summer of friendship without passion. But suddenly the vision is shattered, the spell is broken, for he sees that he wants her only because she is the embodiment of dead love; in her the ghosts of past passions have found substance. Now he realises this, any sort of relationship is impossible.

*v.*12. *Penelope, Ulysses:* he thinks of Ulysses, after his wanderings, settling down with Penelope to a contented old age.

122. FERISHTAH'S FANCIES: PROLOGUE 1884

Ferishtah is the name of a seventeenth-century Persian historian, and his name is the only thing about him which Browning took for this series of poems. Characteristic of his later manner, these poems are cryptic, colloquial and staccato in style. In the Prologue he explains how he mixes the essence of his poems, the thought, with varied images and fancies to make it more palatable, just as a cook mixes the flavours in his dishes.

*l.*1. *ortolans:* 'the garden bunting, a small bird esteemed as a table delicacy' (Oxford Dictionary).

*l.*4. *lyre with spit:* standing for poetry and cookery.

l.23.   *quince:* hard, acid fruit.
l.36.   *gormandising:* eating gluttonously.
l.38.   *Gressoney:* a village in the Alps, where the poem was written.

123.   DUBIETY   1889
   This, like the remaining poems, is from Browning's final volume
Asolando, published on the day of Browning's death, December 12th,
1889. The volume consists of a series of mainly short lyrics in a mood
of gentle and reminiscent meditation. The remembrance of his life with
Elizabeth was very close to him. The title of the volume was derived
from the name of the little town of Asolo, near Venice, where he
spent some of his last months, and which he had loved in his youth.

124.   NOW   1889

125.   POETICS   1889
   He is content to think of his love simply as herself and not in terms
of conventional romantic images.

125.   SUMMUM BONUM   1889

126.   A PEARL, A GIRL   1889

126.   SPECULATIVE   1889

127.   INAPPREHENSIVENESS   1889
l.4.   *Yonder, the ruin:* i.e. of the palace of Queen Cornaro, who, exiled
from Cyprus, lived at Asolo, with Cardinal Bembo acting as Secretary.
(Note to 1905 edition.)
l.16.   *distent:* distended—that is, fixed on the horizon, not on the man
at her side.
l.34.   *Vernon Lee:* pseudonym of Violet Paget, a writer on art and
other subjects, whose work might have been confused with Ruskin's
on this occasion.

128.   EPILOGUE TO 'ASOLANDO'   1889
   This is Browning's last poem, and his own epitaph on himself. He
retains to the end his colloquial and cryptic style, and his meaning,
though clear enough in general, is not easy to disentangle in detail, as
the following attempt at a paraphrase will indicate:

'When at midnight your thoughts wander freely, will they turn to me who once loved you and was loved in return? And will you pity me lying in the grave, which fools think a prison?

'How I loved, how I was loved, and how I was misunderstood! When I was living, what had I to do with sluggards and sentimentalists? Was I one to drivel like a pessimist with no object in life? What was I like?

'I believed in fighting and striving; I was an optimist and never expected the triumph of evil; I considered that setbacks and hardships are sent to strengthen our resolution; and I believed in immortality.

'No, in the very midst of your daily toil, greet the unknown future with enthusiasm. Urge men to march forward, each of their faculties braced to its true purpose. Exhort them to ever greater efforts, in the future as in the present.'

INDEX OF TITLES AND FIRST LINES